MANIFESTO OF COMMON SENSE

Bruce C. Rosetto

Milton Rae Press
An Imprint of Morgan James Publishing

Manifesto of Common Sense

Copyright © 2010 Bruce C. Rosetto. All rights reserved.

No part of this publication may be reproduced or transmitted in any form or by any means, mechanical or electronic, including photocopying and recording, or by any information storage and retrieval system, without permission in writing from the author or publisher (except by a reviewer, who may quote brief passages and/or short brief video clips in a review.)

Disclaimer: The Publisher and the Author make no representations or warranties with respect to the accuracy or completeness of the contents of this work and specifically disclaim all warranties, including without limitation warranties of fitness for a particular purpose. No warranty may be created or extended by sales or promotional materials. The advice and strategies contained herein may not be suitable for every situation. This work is sold with the understanding that the Publisher is not engaged in rendering legal, accounting, or other professional services. If professional assistance is required, the services of a competent professional person should be sought. Neither the Publisher nor the Author shall be liable for damages arising herefrom. The fact that an organization or website is referred to in this work as a citation and/or a potential source of further information does not mean that the Author or the Publisher endorses the information the organization or website may provide or recommendations it may make. Further, readers should be aware that internet websites listed in this work may have changed or disappeared between when this work was written and when it is read.

ISBN 978-0-98207-503-6

Library of Congress Control Number: 2009943420

MILTON RAE
PRESS

Milton Rae Press
An Imprint of Morgan James Publishing
1225 Franklin Ave., STE 325
Garden City, NY 11530-1693
Toll Free 800-485-4943
www.MorganJamesPublishing.com

Habitat for Humanity®
Peninsula
Building Partner

In an effort to support local communities, raise awareness and funds, Morgan James Publishing donates one percent of all book sales for the life of each book to Habitat for Humanity. Get involved today, visit www.HelpHabitatForHumanity.org.

Table of Contents

Preface. 1

Chapter One: The Problem. 7

Chapter Two: What Economic Policy do we need to maintain our global competitiveness? How our tax policy and regulatory environment are to blame. 19

Chapter Three: Is American Capitalism Dead? 33

Chapter Four: How do we shape our Energy Policy to further the ability of our country to maintain its economic and military superiority? 49

Chapter Five: The Importance of Free Trade. 57

Chapter Six: What must we do from a national security perspective to maximize the safety of security of our country and what role our military must play to assist in achieving this goal? 61

Chapter Seven: Why our children must get a world class education 65

Chapter Eight: How Social Security has sucked the wealth out of our senior citizens and caused them to be dependent on government rather than independent. 71

Chapter Nine: Back to the Economy—The Truth behind who caused the 2008 Financial Crisis. 75

Chapter Ten: Immigration Must be Solved 85

Chapter Eleven: Healthcare 91

Chapter Twelve:	Healthcare Reform—What This is Really All About	93
Chapter Thirteen:	Why our politicians (of either party) are our enemies in the fight to restore America	111
Chapter Fourteen:	Call to Action	115

Appendix......123

    U.S. Constitution......123

    Bill of Rights and Amendments to U.S. Constitution......147

PREFACE

The title of this book is a play on the "Manifesto of the Communist Party" written in 1848 by Karl Marx and Friedrich Engel in London. The reason I chose this title is because I believe America is becoming a socialist society. Signs of communist tendencies are appearing in more and more of our politicians. Americans may ultimately choose to adopt policies and philosophies that are consistent with the beliefs of Marx and Engel, but they should do so knowingly and with an educated intent of adopting this type of government.

My concern in writing this book is that Americans are being led down this primrose path unknowingly as politicians disguise, and even hide, the consequences of the policies they are pushing on America. Why do I believe this? The Obama administration, specifically, and liberals, generally, have created a real war against capitalism in every policy argument they pursue. "Soak the rich". Americans should have housing, education, retirement, healthcare, and even new fuel efficient cars all paid for by the "rich". The Obama administration advocates that compensation earned by rich people is immoral and their income should be regulated by the political class. The political class strives to control every aspect of our lives: tell us what schools we can go to; how we should think and speak; what health care we are entitled to receive and what procedures our physicians are allowed to perform on us; how much we should earn; what type of car we should drive; what foods we should eat; what type of jobs our young people should be seeking (Obama has said it is okay to be a community activist but told young Americans not to go into finance); religion is irrelevant; inevitable position of the nanny state in our daily lives; continued deterioration and destruction of the American family; and so much more.

The goal of the essays included in this dissertation is to motivate Americans to think about the issues facing our nation, not from the perspective of one political party or another, but rather from a point of view as to what is best for our nation's future. We are all Americans, and most Americans want the same things. We may differ with our approach on how to best achieve the things we want for ourselves, our families, our community, and our nation, but at our core, the majority of Americans agree with the goals of our nation. Most liberals and conservatives agree on much more than they disagree. Most Americans want the same things: a robust and productive economy that remains the ideal of the world; a strong national security program to safeguard our shores from foreign attack; the educational system in the US, from pre-school to post graduate, to be among the top educational systems in the world; a sensible energy program that reduces our dependency on foreign governments; equal opportunity for all of its citizens; and the best healthcare system in the world. Most Americans are compassionate people who take pride in helping their neighbors, their communities and even people from around the world to achieve a better life.

I could go on, but you understand my point. The essays herein are my thoughts on how to achieve the things most Americans want. Whether you agree with my opinions or not, it doesn't matter. We are all united, as Americans and we must be able to debate and discuss our nation's problems in a mature, intelligent way without personal abuse or attacks of those who disagree with us primarily out of a desire of political opposition to destroy lives of people who have a different view. My only request of you is that you respect my opinions, as I will respect the opinions of my fellow countrymen. This is what separates America from most other countries of the world. In Venezuela, Iran, China, Russia, Cuba and many other countries around the world, if you disagree with figures of authority, you may literally disappear. Let's not allow our nation to lose its ability to have strong disagreements on policy differences without the vile and disgusting tactics others employ to advance their policy beliefs on others.

It all comes down to understanding the critical issues facing our country today. Issues, which, if not dealt with in an intelligent way, could end up destroying our country and our standing as the # 1 economy and #1 military power in the world. We must not permit the current decline of our country to continue. We must change the way we do business in order to position ourselves competitively in the world market place. We, the citizens, must

Preface

take control, with a loud voice, to force our politicians to deal with the major issues facing us. If they refuse, then only we, as citizens, can force the change. Our politicians will listen when, and only when, they believe their livelihood will come to an end if they continue to do business as usual. Our politicians, by nature, are weak people who position themselves on the 'direction of the wind' rather than standing up with a strong set of core beliefs of what must be done in order to move our nation forward in ways to achieve the goals we all want. Thus, we, the citizens, must provide the backbone to the spineless personalities of most of our politicians.

There are many topics that I have not included in this conglomeration of essays. I wrote this in essay form because I wanted to keep this brief, easily readable, and focused on topics that are in keeping with the theme of these essays - - maintaining our competitiveness in the world through the strongest capitalist economy in the world and the strongest military in the world. From that foundation, America can achieve its dreams for all of its citizens. If we lose our economic or military status, then nothing else will matter because our nation will not be able to meet our dreams.

We have a tremendous country. We are the envy of the world. We need to keep it this way. We know who we are. We do not want to be like Europe, which has moved too far toward socialism and is now struggling to increase capitalism in order to improve their economies. We have been successful being Americans and we should be proud of that. I am extremely fearful about the future of our country. For the first time in American history we have as many people dependent on government welfare as we have productive Americans. If this scale tips with more dependents than producers in our society, our nation will never recover. It has become socially popular to beat up on, abuse, and take political advantage of the half of our nation that produces our core strength. This is truly scary.

Therefore, we must unite as citizens and take our country back. Our politicians are too busy enriching themselves, focusing on opinion polls, and taking short term views rather than the long term interests of our country. We, the people, can no longer tolerate ignorance, incompetence, selfishness, corruption, and laziness that so many of our politicians exhibit on a much too frequent basis. If we continue to close our eyes, the America our children inherit will be much worse off than the America we were able to enjoy. The time is now. You must get off the couch and do something. I have been guilty of sitting on the couch for too long, but I have come to realize this is no longer acceptable. We must speak out. We must demand results from our politicians, or we must 'fire' them en masse. Your patriotism and love for our country demand that you act, that you be heard, and that you help make a difference.

CHAPTER ONE
THE PROBLEM

Are the glory days of America behind us? It is not too late to change the growing perception that this might be the case, but it requires the resolve of the American people to be accomplished. We are at war, not only against radical Islam and the forces of terrorism, but, more importantly, we are in an economic war that reflects directly on the ability of the United States to maintain its economic superpower status in the world. If we lose our status as the #1 economic superpower, life in America will change in ways we cannot even begin to imagine. If I appear pessimistic, it is because I believe the American people have become apathetic and woefully uninformed as to the impact the policies being supported by our political class will have on the ability of America to prosper, lead the world, and continue to enrich our citizens in values, health, financial circumstances and just about every other method of measurement. Perhaps Americans have willingly allowed themselves to be misinformed because we have allowed ourselves to become obese and lazy and are no longer the lean and mean machine that built this country. We are at a historical crossroads that can determine whether America continues to lead the world or finds that it is a nation on decline. (Actually, despite the appearance of this opening paragraph I am very optimistic that Americans will rally to the cause like they have done throughout history every time they have been faced with travesty or world events that challenge our way of life. Americans just need to realize that once again we are in that fight for our futures.)

The problem is that America is losing the race to maintain its #1 status on global competiveness and, when we lose our economic superiority, our military prowess and national security will follow. Our lifestyle, our wealth, our freedom, our security, our desire to improve education or health care, everything we take for granted (and we Americans do take everything for granted!) will decline correspondingly with our economic superiority. Our future greatness starts and ends with us maintaining our economic superiority.

Fact: The International Tax Rankings for 2008 show the United States as having the second highest tax rate on American corporations in the world. The second highest! Well, not entirely true, if your company is located in states like California, New York, New Jersey, Pennsylvania and other such high havens for taxing business, then your company has the privilege of living under the highest tax burden in the world.

Fact: The communist country of China is more capitalist than the United States. It is truly frightening that capitalism is making new millionaires in places like China, Russia and India on a daily basis while the United States is falling behind. Moscow has more millionaires than any other city in the world.

Fact: A billion new consumers are coming on line in the next two decades in China, and perhaps a billion plus when India and other developing nations are included. These new consumers will change the world. Their purchasing power will increase the wealth of many nations, which is certainly a good thing, but it will mean all commodity prices will go up. Gold, oil, natural gas, silver, copper, food, lumber, and concrete are a few examples. All these markets will have substantial price increases in the coming decades and will result in geopolitical changes. The impact of this is still very uncertain.

Fact: Our government committed itself to spend more money in the first 60 days of the new administration over the next ten years than the United States has spent in its entire history. Spending increased significantly during the Bush administration as well, but he had a worldwide war on terror going on. Our government is now spending trillions of dollars without having a clue as to how it will affect our nation's future. We are becoming a debtor nation dependent on countries, like China, just so we can afford to finance our tremendous debt. This is ridiculous! We are depending on China to secure our future. What happens to our economy when our nation needs to finance its future debt obligations, now estimated at $800 billion per year just to pay interest on our debt, and China refuses to be our lender? Do we declare bankruptcy? Do we suffer hyper-inflation and devalue our dollar? Do we lose our standing in the world? Just imagine we need China's assistance to deal with a nuclear threat from

The Problem

North Korea or Iran. We may have lost the ability to influence China's behavior because we are in a debtor position to them!

Liberals in America will be pleased for they believe, at their core, that America is the problem. If our economic and military superiority decline, then the rest of the world will simply leave us alone and we could have a liberal utopia where our government redistributes the wealth and be able to spend money on every program the liberal intellectual elites dream up so that no citizen has any pain in any aspect of their lives – literally from cradle to grave the government would take care of every need. The government would be responsible for assuring equality of wealth and lifestyles, which they believe would make the world a better place. The problem is that we already know this won't work. Russia, China, Cuba and even parts of Europe have tried this path and they have grudgingly acknowledged that capitalism is needed or their economies go stagnant, their people go hungry, and the quality of life, from the education of their children, to healthcare, to the ability of their people to enjoy any leisure time similar to what American families enjoy, is just not supportable. Western Europe has largely become socialist in its policies, and the governments and their people have realized that there are limits to how far socialism can go before being forced back to capitalist policies. Western Europe has turned to more conservative principles for the first time in decades. When Europeans get sick, they come to the United States for medical care if they can afford to. Some of the strongest growth areas in Europe are from some of the former Soviet bloc countries, as well as countries like Ireland, that have unleashed pro-growth policies, low taxes, and reduced regulation.

Frankly, if America was no longer the umbrella protecting Western Europe, their countries and lifestyle would decline even more than they already have in the last 40 years. Radical Islam will ravage European cities and Russia will invade Ukraine, and other former Soviet bloc countries, to garner the wealth these countries have developed since the fall of the Soviet empire. China, Russia, Iran, North Korea, Venezuela, and other nations ruled by despots will create a true axis of evil to mold the world into a place in which they will dictate terms to the United States and Europe, and we will be too weak economically and militarily to do anything about it. In fact, we will be in so much debt to them that we will be pleading for them to leave us alone and stop bullying us, at which point they will torment us even more.

China is expanding itself economically; positioning itself to far surpass the United States. China is making deal after deal with countries in Africa and South America in order to gain control of the vast natural resources possessed by these countries. They are building energy plants at the rate of one per week. Nuclear power plants, coal plants, and even huge wind farms. China is on the move and is planning for economic dominance in the world. The United States has not built a nuclear power plant in decades, even though nuclear power plants provides the cheapest long-term energy usage of any energy alternatives and has the lowest carbon emissions.

China is currently financing the debt of the United States. This will end, but not at a time that will benefit the United States. You can be sure that it will end when it is in the best interests of China to pull the plug. Meanwhile, the Chinese are now dictating to our

The Problem

Treasury Department that we need to adopt policies to decrease the enormous deficit the Obama administration is creating. In other words, the Chinese are demanding that the U.S. either cut spending significantly, or increase taxes significantly. Which one of these options do you think the Obama administration and the fools in Congress will adopt? The Chinese are talking about the world adopting a new world currency and it will no longer be the U.S. dollar. I am hopeful that Americans will come to realize that we cannot afford the policies promoted by the socialists and communists currently running our governments at the federal, state and local level, and they will take the action needed to re-establish fiscal health to our country.

The fact that President Obama does not believe in capitalism is a blatant truth. He is at best a socialist. At times he thinks even more like a communist. It is frightening, but true. In 2008, America elected radicals to run our government. We are now paying the price in ways we may not understand for a decade, or longer. By then it will be too late to correct the devastation to America's economy and its position as the world's lone superpower.

The simple reality is that America is despised by our intellectual elite and American haters throughout the world. Our strength is what has kept the peace in the world. It's not just our military strength, but, and more importantly, our economic strength. It is only due to our economic strength that we can afford a strong military presence where needed to protect us, and the rest of the civilized countries around the world, from the frightening forces out there. The problem is that the people who want to hurt us and other civilized countries, gain new knowledge everyday and create more dangerous weapons to destroy us. How long will it be before some of these crazies poison our water supply, cut off our oil supplies, attack our computer systems to shut down commerce and trade, or send nuclear weapons to our cities?

When we lose our economic strength, our military strength will weaken and the world will be a dangerous place. Do you remember how we won the Cold War with Russia? It was credited to a massive build up in our military. This was able to be accomplished because we were much stronger economically and Russia could simply not afford to keep up. Their effort to keep up risked bankrupting their country, to the point where they could not maintain their 'iron hand' over their people. Russia learned its lesson and has since allowed unbridled capitalism to rebuild their economic strength, and now Putin is using this to rebuild his country's military power.

Most Americans are proud of our status as #1 in the world, whether it is in strength of our economy, our military, our productivity, our wealth, even the number of medals we win at the Olympics. Unfortunately, more and more Americans seem to think that being #1 is not that important. Every fiber of my soul shakes in fear at the thought that Americans may not care, and don't completely understand the consequences that will befall their lives, and the lives of their children, if we continue down our current path.

It should come as no surprise to Americans that our country has continued a migration to the left in its policies and politics over the last four decades. I believe that if Franklin Delano Roosevelt were running for President today he would be considered a right wing Republican. Our current politicians strive to make America like Western Europe, yet Western European countries have been in a state of economic and military decline for decades. Why would we want to follow their model? The answer is simple. Our politicians have one primary goal: to get re-elected. In order to do that, they need to continually give new things to the people in every election. They tell people they have a "right" to everything they offer. Heck, we all like free stuff, but the problem is that nothing is ever free. The problem is that giving things to people costs money. The more money we take out of the system, the more our economic superiority is damaged. Our politicians monitor daily polls to determine how they should think, how they should govern, and, even worse, how to convey their messages to the public to "convince" them that their policies are correct. Yet, if you look at history, the most successful politicians in history have been leaders who take a long term view – 10, 20, or even 30 years into the future. When a leader takes a long term view, they are generally detested by the electorate while they serve their term. Truman was very unpopular when he left office at the end of his term. Today he is considered one of our finest Presidents. Reagan was all but crucified by the liberals while he served. Now even liberals will admit that he was a good President. Lincoln was despised when he served; even by people within his party. He now sits at the mantel as one of our greatest Presidents.

Democrats have control of the White House and the Congress for 2009 and 2010. Democrats have decided to fight terrorism with standard police powers, rather than military powers.

Manifesto of Common Sense

The Democrats have an overwhelming desire to be "liked" by everyone in the world. In speech after speech after speech, President Obama has apologized to the world, time and again, for our being, well, Americans. As his administration makes instrumental changes to prove to the world how "nice" we are, and put into place policy changes designed to make the world love us, they are laying the seeds for disaster. What if during the first term of President Obama a terrorist attack occurs? People will realize that Bush had kept us safe during his tenure. People will realize this was not a coincidence, but a result of enormous hard work behind the scenes and under the radar screen in places around the world that Americans don't even know exist or have even heard of. Americans will clamor to go back to the period of President Bush for he kept our country safe for seven years post 9/11. I predict that President Bush will be considered more favorably in the future than he is currently. He fought the war on terror as a war, not like Clinton who fought it with police powers or like Obama who is now following the Clinton model. People will remember that the surge in Iraq worked and tens of millions of people were freed from tyranny. Iraq is enjoying some democratic success. America will be attacked by terrorists in the future. It is not a question of "if", but "when". Policies do make a difference. It is hard to imagine now that history will be kind to George W. Bush, but I believe that is a real possibility. Bush had a long term view of what is best for America , unlike his predecessor who was more focused on the daily tracking polls. It will be interesting to see which President historians will ultimately think was the more successful.

The Problem

What can we do as countrymen to ensure we remain competitive in the global marketplace? How do we ensure our economy remains strong so that we can pass on an even higher quality of life to our children?

Let's face it, whether Democrat, Republican, Libertarian, or whatever, we all want the same basic things in life. We want a high quality of life. We want our children to be well educated. We want to enjoy some of the finer things in life during our leisure time, from eating out at nice restaurants to being able to take a terrific family vacation, purchasing the latest electronic gadgets, attending sports events, etc. We want more leisure time. We want the best health care system in the world. We want to save for our retirement so we can actually afford to enjoy retirement some day. We want to live in peace and be safe in our streets. We want to live in a free society. We want to prosper and we want our neighbors to prosper. We want our children to have an even better life than we enjoy.

The difference between our political philosophies really amounts to what is the best way to achieve our desires and dreams. This manifesto is simply my view of policies we MUST adhere to if we want to have the best chance to have our dreams fulfilled.

If we are unsuccessful in restraining our government's out of control spending, our ballooning deficits, and continuing destruction of the capitalist tendencies that have built this country over the last two hundred years, then I suggest the following: Buy oil, natural gas, gold, copper, silver and real estate. Short the US Dollar. Hopefully this investment strategy will create enough wealth to you as an individual that you can withstand the high inflation and low growth economy President Obama is unleashing on America. I estimate this will occur commencing in 2011 unless we radically change course from his current economic plan. If Americans are stupid enough to elect even more radicals to our government in 2010, then I suggest you take your money and leave the country before President Obama and his radical Pelosi led Congress take it all away from you. Between Obama, Pelosi, Rangel, Waxman and so many others, be prepared for aggregate tax rates of 70% if you earn more than $250,000 per year. We are almost there now. Think I am kidding, read the next chapter.

CHAPTER TWO
WHAT ECONOMIC POLICY DO WE NEED TO MAINTAIN OUR GLOBAL COMPETITIVENESS? HOW OUR TAX POLICY AND REGULATORY ENVIRONMENT ARE TO BLAME.

As indicated in the prior chapter, it cannot be over emphasized how important it is to the United States, and the western way of life, that we maintain our economic superiority in the world. During the Bush administration, the economy of the United States had actually performed much better than the media had reported. The U.S. economy grew during the Bush administration at a healthier rate than any other western nation, and, according to the International Tax Institute, one of the primary reasons for this sustained strong growth was tax cuts. Hmmm, tax cuts.

Whether in Ireland, Germany, Japan, or anywhere else in the world for that matter, reducing the tax burden has always produced strong economic growth. In the United States during the Kennedy,

Reagan and Bush administrations, tax cuts produced increased wealth to all Americans by improving a growing economy. It appears that most of our current politicians do not understand this simple principle. Too many of our politicians have a goal not to create individual wealth, but to create a socialist society. There is no reward for entrepreneurs, creativity, productivity, risk taking, or other beneficial behaviors. These are alien to their concept of a society where every person has equal things, regardless of how little or how hard they work. The core of the liberal philosophy is that every individual is "entitled" to everything the rich have, regardless of the effort the rich have made to acquire such things. The problem is that if you take away the incentive for people to produce more, create more, or take risks in order to get more than their rivals, then society becomes stagnant and declines because the wealth of the nation, and all of its citizens, has been taken away. Liberals live in a fantasy world. They believe there is no end to how much they can take from the producers in society to pass on to the non-producers, and still expect the nation will be able to afford their grand social agenda. Margaret Thatcher, the former prime minister of the United Kingdom, once said that socialism is wonderful, until you run out of people to pay for it. This is the precipice America now stands on and, with the trillions of dollars of new spending Obama and Pelosi are planning for America, it won't be long before there won't be any Americans who can afford to pay for the productivity destructive socialist plans they are forcing on us.

There is no magic to creating a strong economy whereby all citizens can aspire to greatness, grab the American dream and thus propel the economy of the nation to new heights. It requires our politicians, however, to work together and put behind them their need and desire to continually promise new and ever expanding government programs. Politicians have created a society where the voters are treated as crack addicts. With every election they entice voters with more and more grandiose ideas and convince voters that they can get more for less. Every election offers promises that won't be kept because the programs are not affordable. In every election the politicians dupe voters. And the process proliferates. For this reason, I propose that our nation institute term limits at every level of government. We would get people who are willing to serve our country for the right reasons, and are then obligated to return to the private world after 2 or 3 terms where they actually have to earn a living like the rest of us.

Here is what politicians need to do. (Every time in history when these policies have been followed, the results have been a growing economy):

1. Reduce the tax burden as a percentage of the Gross Domestic Product. Make the Bush tax cuts permanent, which had led the US economy to be among the strongest in the world for seven years at a time when terrorism threatened our way of life, the Iraq War ballooned military spending, and commodity prices sky rocketed due to unprecedented consumer demand in developing nations. With all of these enormous pressures on our economy, we should have experienced a declining economy and wealth base, yet the facts prove the opposite. Naturally, the liberals and media outlets refused to recognize the

strong gains of our economy and created a contradictory image because they always put their politics ahead of the best interests of the people and the country.

2. The United States should follow the lead of most industrialized nations today by eliminating or greatly reducing the tax burden on corporations. The greatest lie of the century is to believe that corporations pay taxes that will relieve the individual of his or her tax obligation. Taxes on corporations are literally a hidden tax on individuals for all taxes imposed on a corporation are passed through to the consumer in the price of their services and goods. When you buy food, gas, clothes, toys, houses, or whatever, the corporate tax burden is already built into the pricing structure. As an example, when gas was over $4.00 per gallon, the politicians branded the oil companies as evil profiteers, but did you know our government makes more money on each gallon from the taxes on the oil than the oil industry earns? Of course not! The government taxes are hidden.

Most nations now recognize that corporate taxes are merely a hidden tax on individuals. If all taxes were assessed on the one and only true payer of taxes, the individual, the government would lose its ability to easily increase taxes in other avenues because the tax burden would be transparent to the individual. Our politicians talk about offering transparency but, in reality, they are masters at playing hide-and-seek with the voter. They have layered the tax code with so many levels of taxes that it is impossible for ordinary people to determine how much of their pay actually goes to taxes. If the voters had a clue of their true taxation, there would be a revolution in this country that would make the Boston tea party look tame. Many people in this country pay more than half of their income in taxes of one sort or another, and in some states that tax burden can exceed 60% of their income. But people have no clue to this reality for the politicians mask the truth at every step and disguise it so that people think someone else is paying the tax. Pay attention to the health care reform legislation. It will cost over a trillion dollars and will be paid mostly by hidden taxes so Americans can't see how much free healthcare is really going to cost them.

Here are just a few of the taxes that we pay that most individuals don't consider:

Corporate taxes

State Franchise fees

License fees (is there a business in America today that doesn't have to pay a license fee, whether you are a barber, trash collector, or anything else?)

Fuel Taxes

Road taxes

Tolls

Impact fees (in most communities, impact fees have doubled, and even tripled, in recent years thus driving the cost of home building higher. This means when a new home is purchased, the price is thousands of dollars higher to include the impact fees, but no consumer recognizes this when they buy the house. The high prices are blamed on the developer, and that is exactly what our politicians want to have believed.)

School taxes

Service charges

Life insurance premiums (yes, life insurance is a form of hidden tax. Due to the fact that we pay taxes when we work and save our money, and then have to pay taxes again when we die on whatever we accumulate during our life, many in our country are "forced" to have life insurance just so there is cash available to pay the tax man when we die. Otherwise families would be forced to sell their businesses, farms or other assets just to pay death taxes, and this is after paying heavy taxes their whole life.)

Agency fees

Regulatory fees and fines. (Most government agencies today work like mini-profit centers. They find new and creative ways to charge businesses that they regulate, and then impose heavy fines and penalties if a business has even the slightest error or misjudgment. Compliance fines can be very expensive but a great way for government agencies to fund their budgets, so more and more regulatory inspectors act like police agents and raid small businesses with the intent to "find" compliance issues just so they can impose big fines. They then go back to their offices and adopt new policies and regulations so they can go back to the business at a later date and hit them with even more fines and penalties.)

Transfer taxes
Intangible taxes
Tourism taxes

Then of course there are the taxes that are more evident:

Payroll taxes
Social Security taxes
Estate taxes
Real Estate Taxes
Sales taxes
City taxes
County taxes
State Taxes
Municipal fees

And then there are a slew of new taxes coming, but President Obama and Congress will call them something other than a "tax". For example, surcharges that must be paid by Americans who have "cadillac" health plans or fees imposed on taxpayers who refuse to participate in the new healthcare plan being forced upon them. There will be assessments against doctors, insurance companies, hospitals and others who are a part of healthcare system to drive the behavior our government wants. All of this will serve to drive up the cost of insurance premiums for healthcare, which in turn, will be used by our government as an excuse to accelerate the drive toward a single payer healthcare system. Meanwhile, none of these charges, assessments, fines, penalties, etc will be labeled a "tax".

Our tax system needs to be thrown out and re-written to simplify the process and at the same time generate more tax revenue. This will be discussed in greater detail later, but I am a strong proponent of a flat tax. The bottom line is that when you levy all of these taxes on the economy, it creates a drag that makes us less competitive in the global market, plus it creates a situation where most Americans, (at least those that work), pay more than 50% of their income to taxes whether they realize or not.

This representation of taxes paid is no exaggeration. Take for example a middle class American spouse who jointly earn $250,000 per annum. Our government will claim they are rich, but if they live on the East Coast or the West Coast of America, the $250,000 per year will support a family living in a middle-class house in a middle-class neighborhood, drive a middle-class car and, maybe, go on vacation with once a year and stay in a middle-class hotel. This family is taxed 39% at the federal level. If they live in the northeast or the west coast, their state is taking another 7-13% of their income, bringing their tax rate near or above 50%. If they work in the city, they are also paying a few more points of their pay to the city government. Now add school and real property tax, sales tax, gas tax, tolls when they commute to work, government agency fees every time they use a government agency, and social security taxes contributing another few percentage points against their income. It is difficult to calculate in the 'hidden' taxes you don't see, like all business taxes and impact fees assessed on companies which are built into the prices of the products and services they offer. 60% is conservatively on the low side of what many Americans are paying in overall taxes. The fortunate few in the top 1% of American earners will be burdened with new tax surcharges, loss of tax credits and other assessments by the Obama administration and their tax burden will easily top out at 65%-70% of their income.

We need to demand that our government lift the veil so we can see how much is really paid in taxes, at all levels. This would be true transparency. Barack Obama campaigned heavily on the transparency issue but, once in office, his administration has gone to great lengths to ensure there has been no transparency. He does not want Americans to understand how much of their income really goes to taxes. Those facts, if known to the public, would truly create a revolution in this country.

3. Streamline government bureaucracy. The bureaucracy we have in place is its own form of tax on the American economy. This is not to imply that we do not need regulation of industry and businesses because we do. What it does mean, though, is that an audit of each and every government program should be taken to measure and analyze what is necessary and what is not. Our bureaucracies never go away, even when the need they served dissipates. Bureaucracies are self-fulfilling prophecies. They find reasons to exist, grow, and spend money, despite what may actually be going on in the real world. Have you ever seen a government program go away? Have you ever seen a government office that is overstaffed? In order to be competitive in the world marketplace, our government needs to find ways to regulate itself in a more efficient manner and reduce the costs on business, while maintaining legitimate responsibilities. Politicians, however, like bureaucracy. It

gives them something to hide behind and blame when things don't work right. It is a place that they can reward patronage from constituents who have helped them to get elected.

4. Strengthen the US Dollar. It is important to the flow of capital into the United States, and to the underlying strength of our economy that we maintain a strong dollar policy. In the short term this can hurt our export trade, but in the long run it provides a much sounder economic base. Notwithstanding this fact, our government is intentionally deflating the US Dollar. Yes, I said intentionally. This is one of those dirty little Washington secrets. Our government has become a debtor nation due to decades of socialist policies. In the future, we can look forward to trillion dollar per year deficits as far out as the eye can see. We have been borrowing money from countries like China to support our addiction to more and more social policies. These social policies must be paid for. You either pay for social policies by raising taxes or by cutting other government programs. Congress does not have a good track record for cutting spending, and although Congress is very good at raising taxes (or do we call them fees now), it does its best to disguise the tax increase or minimize its direct effect on the consumer so as to minimize the anger of voters in the next election. So as our country goes into further and further debt each year, we must somehow pay for the shortfall in cash to pay our bills. Thus we borrow money from countries that

produce surpluses of cash, China being the most obvious example. The thing about borrowing money however, is that one day you have to pay it back. We all know how painful that can be. America is worried about its ability to pay back its lenders because it has borrowed so much and is about to borrow historical levels of new debt. The solution in the eyes of our socialist politicians – reduce the value of the dollar and flood dollars into the market to keep our economy "seemingly" healthy. The result WILL BE inflation. Thus, we will pay back our lenders with future dollars that have less value. Get it. We can't afford to pay back the debt we borrowed with the current value of the dollar, so we deflate the dollar and pay our creditors back with cheaper dollars in the future. Now, you understand why China, Russia, and the Arab oil countries are having secret meetings to discuss abolishing the use of US dollars as the international currency for purchasing oil. These countries understand they are being "gamed" by the US and will not put up with it. They will dump the dollar for international purposes taking away the strength America gets from being the world's reserve currency. America's leadership in the world then becomes a thing of the past. Are the socialists happy yet?

5. Achieve Energy independence. This is critical to the success of our economy. We are redistributing $700 billion dollars annually to other countries. We need to keep that money home. Building nuclear power plants, coal plants, drilling for oil, manufacturing jobs for new technologies,

engineering and management jobs that go along with creating new industries based on solar, wind, hydrogen, natural gas and other alternative energy sources will bolster our economy for decades to come. We cannot depend on the Middle East and Russia for the energy we need, or we might find out we have become a second rate country over night. By the way, becoming energy independent can also serve to save the US dollar and maintain the US as the globally dominant force it has been.

6. Educate our Children. The long term success of our economy is undeniably intertwined with properly educating our children. We cannot compete in the global market place if our children are not prepared. The public education system in the United States is doing a dismal job of educating our children. Compare the education of our children to the rest of the world, and our results are not impressive. Graduating high school does not begin to ready our children for the world market. Schools have no discipline. Our school administrators are more worried about being politically correct than educating our children. The number of students who graduate from our high schools without the ability to perform simple math or read and write well is astonishing, and we should be ashamed. The number of our children who leave school thinking the world owes them a high paying job and an easy life is even more astounding. Our students must be motivated to be the most educated and disciplined work force in the world.

7. Free Trade. Statistics do not lie. Examine the result of the free trade pacts we have entered into with Canada, then later under NAFTA, and the results are undeniable. Free trade has not only added wealth to our neighbors in Canada and Mexico, but created enormous wealth and benefits to the United States. In a world that is becoming more competitive, it is important for the United States to not only maintain and strengthen the current treaties, but to expand them. NAFTA should be expanded to include Latin America and South America. In this way, the Americas will have a trading zone that can, and will successfully compete against China, India, Russia and Europe. As the Americas trade more with each other, the wealth of each and every nation within the trade zone will benefit. As the economies of Latin America develop into sustainable markets, illegal immigration will be much less of an issue. People will not enter the United States illegally if they have an economy that can support their families. You don't see Canadians sneaking into the United States, (although many of them do enjoy spending the winter months in our southern states.) Free trade will destroy dictators like Venezuela's Chavez. Growing economies in Colombia, Brazil, Peru and other South American nations will unravel the strangle hold the dictators of South America have placed on their people.

CHAPTER THREE
IS AMERICAN CAPITALISM DEAD?

As a country, we are being led far afield from a capitalist society. I believe Americans remain strongly capitalist. However, the leaders we have elected to run our country clearly think differently. The majority of Congress today leans socialist in its political beliefs. Those individuals at the pinnacle of power, President Obama, Nancy Pelosi, Henry Waxman, Barbara Boxer and others are the most left leaning of the Democrat Party that has itself swerved to the left over the last decade.

Our country has witnessed a huge difference between how President Obama speaks when delivering a prepared speech versus his 'off the cuff' remarks, which tend to reveal his true feelings. Joe, the Plumber, was thrown into fame during the presidential campaign of 2008 by getting then Senator Obama to reveal his real thoughts about redistributing wealth in America. Since then, his political advisors have worked diligently to ensure President Obama reads from the teleprompter in an effort to keep him focused on the scripted message, playing 'hide-and-seek' with Americans about the truth of what he really believes.

Yet, his rhetoric is usually great. He is a fabulous orator when reading from a script. I can't help enjoying his speeches, even though I realize he is often dishonest about his real intentions and beliefs. I even remember hearing a speech on television on July 11, 2009 that startled me when I heard it as I could not believe the words were spoken by President Obama. The part of the speech that caught my attention is as follows:

> *Governments that respect the will of their own people, that govern by consent and not coercion, are more prosperous, they are more stable and more successful than governments that do not.*
>
> *This is about more than just holding elections. It's also about what happens between elections. Repression can take many forms, and too many nations, even those that have elections, are plagued by problems that condemn their people to poverty. No country is going to create wealth if its leaders exploit the economy to enrich themselves ... No business wants to invest in a place where the government skims 20 percent off the top ... That is not democracy, that is tyranny, even if occasionally you sprinkle an election in there. And now is the time for that style of governance to end.*
>
> *In the 21st century, capable, reliable and transparent institutions are the key to success—... an independent press; a vibrant private sector; ... Those are the things that give life to democracy, because that is what matters in people's everyday lives.*

He is right, but how ironic. These truths, as he spoke them, are okay for poor countries, like Ghana, where he delivered this speech. But obviously his attitude at home is different. I, too, believe that what happens between elections is important. I, too, believe that bad government can plague a nation with poverty. I, too, believe skimming 20% off the top of what businesses generate will have adverse effects on the ability of the economy to achieve its maximum growth potential, and thereby lift the greatest number of people out of poverty. I, too, believe that a government that fails to deliver transparent institutions to give its masses a chance at developing legitimate businesses that grow, prosper, and create wealth for the entire nation, is a government of tyranny, not democracy.

For the United States, he believes taxing American businesses at 40% is okay. He believes taxing individuals at 39.5% is fair, and it is even more fair to place a 5% surcharge on wealthy Americans to contribute to the massive healthcare reform plan he wants. He believes doubling natural gas prices and electric bills for homeowners in America is okay when done in the name of a climate change bill that everyone knows will likely have little or no effect on climate change. He believes that bankrupting the American economy in the name of a false stimulus program so that every Democrat can squeeze pet projects that have nothing at all to do with stimulating the economy, can be put in place. He believes that violating basic tenets of contract law, which have stood in all of our history, can be discarded so that his union friends can benefit at the expense of secured creditors who had risked capital. When the secured creditors objected to these violations of law, he threatened IRS audits on their hedge funds in order to silence them. Sounds like fascism to me! The hedge funds caved to his demands, so they must have felt the same way.

He believes that 'his' government can order one of the largest banks in America (Bank of America) to buy out one of the largest securities firms (Merrill Lynch) in America, even though the bank's CEO realized it was not a transaction that was in the best interests of the shareholders of the bank, but because the securities firm was in much more financial trouble then had been realized. He believes that if the CEO (Ken Lewis) of this bank hadn't caved to his demands, it would be fine to threaten the bank with strict audits from the federal banking regulators; A.K.A. threatening the bank's ability to survive. Again, sounds like fascism to me. Ken Lewis must have felt the fascist pressure because he caved and Bank of America went ahead and bought Merrill Lynch.

If this is not an example of fascism, then I don't know what is. I would have expected this behavior from the Germany government in the 1930's or from the communist governments in Russia, China and Venezuela today. I am frightened that such abuse of United States governmental power would happen in my lifetime. This behavior is tyrannical in every sense of the word. But why should I be surprised? After all, he learned how to be a politician in Chicago.

Obama believes that our current tax code, which has 60% of Americans who pay virtually no tax and, therefore, the remaining, and productive, 40% can deliver all sorts of societal freebies to the bottom 60%, is a 'fair' system. He believes this needs to be made even more fair; meaning the 40% of our country that pay taxes must dig deeper into their pockets and pay even higher taxes, so the bottom 60% of our country can get even more free stuff from our government. It is no wonder he won 52% of the vote in the presidential election! Anyone in the 60% of America that receives the handouts and yet pays no tax would naturally vote for him. He certainly did not get votes from anyone who believes that the others have to get off the government dole and pay their own way.

American capitalism is dead as long as President Obama is in office. He has Nancy Pelosi by his side to ramrod their redistributing American wealth idea through government legislation until there is no more wealth to redistribute. Yet President Obama realizes that small developing countries, like Ghana, will only develop strong, vibrant economies through strong democratic governments with transparent institutions that allow the private sector to realize profits in order to grow their businesses and lift their laborers up the economic ladder. But here, in the US, President Obama believes that we don't need profits and a vibrant private sector anymore since there is too much wealth, as compared to the rest of the world, and thus it is his job to redistribute the wealth as he sees fit.

President Obama is attacking American capitalism in every sector. He has nationalized the auto industry for the benefit of his unions. He has nationalized the banks and, just as the banks try to repay the bailout money to escape some of the heavy regulatory hand of our government, the government has sought to change their rules in order to make it more difficult for the banks to repay the bailout money. He is seeking to nationalize the entire financial sector through enormous new regulations. Yet he has left Fannie Mae and Freddie Mac, the two government supported institutions that created the great recession of 2008-2009, to move on without further regulatory oversight. He has nationalized one of the largest insurance companies in the world, AIG. He is seeking to control the compensation of executives throughout many industries, and, if he gets his way, will expand the industries and therefore limits the ability of US citizens to grow their wealth. He demands free healthcare as a way to nationalize 20% of the American economy, and demands control of the salaries doctors, nurses and everyone else in the industry makes. At the same time, government payrolls are exploding. Soon more Americans will be controlled by the government than in the private sector.

Obama is seeking to re-invent America in a most profound way. Any state that does not go along with his plan is threatened with loss of funding. The United States is at our tipping point. He knows it and is trying to push us off the cliff.

Once we fall into socialism, it is over. Obama will have won and destroyed America in the process.

All basic elements of life in America will be completely controlled by the government. 'Free' education. 'Free' healthcare. 'Free' retirement. Where does it end? I need a new car, so how about a free car? Wait a second, our new government motors is actually doing this. The 'Cash for Clunker' program …Now that our government owns Chrysler, it promised every tax payer they can get $4,500 if they buy a new Chrysler with better gas mileage than the existing 'clunker' currently driven, but just like our government to promise a free $4500 to everyone but intentionally neglect to let its citizens know that they have to pay tax on the $4500. There is more. If they acted immediately, Chrysler would match that with another $4,500. Add it up, $9,000 of taxpayer money to be given to anyone who decides to buy a new car! What a great place America is! Everything anyone needs is delivered by the government, so why does anyone need to get up early in the morning, work 12 hours a day, and stress themselves to the point of getting an ulcer? One might as well sit home and let the government take care of them because, by the time the government is done taxing one for the trillions of dollars per year it is now spending, they won't have any money left to enrich themselves or achieve their dreams. What is the point of even trying?

This is the paradox of socialism. Millions of Americans will eventually reach this conclusion and this will put the final nail in the coffin of American capitalism. This is the dream of Liberals in America. It will not be until their dream is achieved that they will realize there is no one left to pay for all of the stuff they promised. By that point, the economies of China and India will rule the world. Goodbye America!

Here are some policy directives dictated by Marx and Engel in the Manifesto of the Communist Party (remember this was written over 160 years ago):

- **Abolition of the family because it only supports capitalism.** Marx and Engel wrote:

    "Abolition of the family! Even the most radical flare up at this infamous proposal of the Communists.

On what foundation is the present family, the bourgeois family, based? On capital, on private gain. In its completely developed form, this family exists only among the bourgeoisie. But this state of things finds its complement in the practical absence of the family among proletarians, and in public prostitution.

The bourgeois family will vanish as a matter of course when its complement vanishes, and both will vanish with the vanishing of capital."

- **State control of education so it can't be used to create more capitalists.** Marx and Engel wrote:

"And your education! Is not that also social, and determined by the social conditions under which you educate, by the intervention direct or indirect, of society, by means of schools, etc.? The Communists have not intended the intervention of society in education; they do but seek to alter the character of that intervention, and to rescue education from the influence of the ruling class."

- **Elimination of privately owned property** (in other words take all property away from rich people who worked hard to accumulate it because they only got rich by taking it from the labor of the working class, and thus government should take it away from the rich and give it back to the workers)

"The distinguishing feature of communism is not the abolition of property generally, but the abolition of bourgeois property. But modern bourgeois private property is the final and most complete expression of the system of producing and

appropriating products that is based on class antagonisms, on the exploitation of the many by the few . . . You are horrified at our intending to do away with private property. . . . In one word, you reproach us with intending to do away with your property. Precisely so; that is just what we intend."

- **Abolition of religion and morality in society.** Marx and Engle wrote:

"But communism abolishes eternal truths, it abolishes all religion, and all morality, instead of constituting them on a new basis; it therefore acts in contradiction to all past historical experience."

Here are some additional thoughts from Marx and Engel worth reading:

"Of course, in the beginning, this cannot be effected except by means of despotic inroads on the rights of property, and on the conditions of bourgeois production; by means of measures, therefore, which appear economically insufficient and untenable, but which, in the course of the movement, outstrip themselves, necessitate further inroads upon the old social order, and are unavoidable as a means of entirely revolutionizing the mode of production."

Nevertheless, in most advanced countries, the following will be pretty generally applicable.

1. Abolition of property in land and application of all rents of land to public purposes.

2. *A heavy progressive or graduated income tax.*
3. *Abolition of all rights of inheritance.*
4. *Confiscation of the property of all emigrants and rebels.*
5. *Centralization of credit in the banks of the state, by means of a national bank with state capital and an exclusive monopoly.*
6. *Centralization of the means of communication and transport in the hands of the state.*
7. *Extension of factories and instruments of production owned by the state; the bringing into cultivation of waste lands, and the improvement of the soil generally in accordance with a common plan.*
8. *Equal obligation of all to work. Establishment of industrial armies, especially for agriculture.*
9. *Combination of agriculture with manufacturing industries; gradual abolition of all the distinction between town and country by a more equable distribution of the populace over the country.*
10. *Free education for all children in public schools. Abolition of children's factory labor in its present form. Combination of education with industrial production, etc."*

This sounds like the change Obama has promised America and that the liberals in the Democratic Party have been espousing for decades. Many of the principles are the same. It is frightening how close the words of Marx and Engle resemble the deeds of our liberal political class. We start with "despotic inroads on the rights of property" (Translation: soak the rich policies) and then we put "conditions on bourgeois production" (Translation:

regulate business with ever growing conditions). These conditions are to be measured by that which will "appear to be economically insufficient and untenable" (Translation: We regulate the business to the point they are not economically viable because we tax their profits to the point where wealth cannot be accumulated). These are the policies that drive the Democrats.

Let's evaluate the core principles discussed my Marx and Engel in light of current policy initiatives of the Democrats.

Abolish property rights. Democrats do this every day. For example: Make insurance companies the villains. Make oil companies the villains. Make pharmaceutical companies the villains. Make Wall Street the villains. Make the rich (defined as anyone who makes more than $250,000 per year) the villains. Make banks the villains. Make hedge funds the villains. By creating class warfare, the Democrats tell the voters, who rarely pay much attention to what is really going on in politics, that they must protect the voters from all of these villains. It is an easy argument and has been incredibly successful in allowing the Democrats to create a bloodless revolution to destroy capitalism and invoke communism. The precepts of communism cannot occur without class warfare, designed to "soak the rich," and take what they have earned to redistribute to those who have not earned it.

A heavy progressive tax. We are already there as the top 1% of Americans pay in excess of 40% of all taxes, the top 10% pay more than 70% of all taxes, and the top 50% pay 97% of all taxes. But Obama has made it clear that he will tax the top 50% of Americans at much higher levels.

Abolition of inheritance rights. We have already adopted this as well. You work hard. You save your money. You pay 35-40% of your income in taxes your whole life. You die. Your estate is then taxed heavily on the amount of money you managed to save upwards of 50% once you get over government set thresholds. If your wealth is tied up in small business or real estate, your family is forced to sell the fruits of your labor in order to pay the tax man. You came into the world with nothing, the liberals believe you should leave the same way, and any wealth they, as the ruling political class, allowed you to keep and accumulate should be redistributed upon your death to people who need it –not your family.

Centralization of banks. We did this. The Federal Reserve was established to centralize banking regulations back in the 1930's. Then, in 2009, we saw the nationalization of the largest banks in our country with the bailout of the banks and the federal government refusing to let the banks pay back the bailout money. Our federal government prefers having control over the banks and, hence, compensation of the bankers.

Centralization of media communications. It appears to me that this goal of Marx and Engle has also been accomplished. When you see 90% of our media actively supporting and promoting the policies of the Democratic Party and the Obama administration, actual ownership of the media by our government is not necessary. Our private media has sold its soul to the left. There are bills in Congress with 'consumer correct' names such as the "Fairness Doctrine," designed for the sole purpose to eradicate free market conditions from radio programs because liberal oriented stations don't seem able to remain financially solvent while conservative oriented radio programs thrive from a financial perspective. A new bill is being offered to force radio stations to focus on local content rather than nationally syndicated shows. Such a bill would eliminate the popular conservative talk show hosts that have their shows nationally syndicated. That, of course, is the whole point of the legislation.

As pointed out earlier, free speech is fine for the liberals; otherwise, the Constitutional right can be regulated against those with a more moderate or conservative viewpoint. Of course, the fact that Americans choose to listen to one broadcast over enough is no longer considered "fair", and therefore Americans would lose one more freedom for the sake of the socialist revolution propounded by the Democratic Party—the right to listen to whatever program on the radio they desire. What happened to our freedoms guaranteed by the U.S. Constitution? The Democrats don't believe in our Constitution, or our Bill of Rights, because, if these documents are read literally, they do not allow the Democrats to do what they want to our country. Do you want gun ownership? Well, the Democrats don't like that, so they ignore what the founding documents of our nation say: they regulate the arms and ammunition industry so as to impair, if not eliminate, this right. If you own a gun, have you bought bullets lately? The price has skyrocketed as a result of forced government mandated policies. Do you believe in free speech? The Democrats are okay with this as long as it the speech supports their beliefs. President Obama is among the worst Presidents ever at dealing with public criticism; any public criticism. He has an office in the White House dedicated to receiving email communications from his supporters to report if they come across any "fishy" communications from their neighbors. (Oh, this is just one more example of how our government is becoming more fascist with every day that Obama and Pelosi are in control!) He has had his staff build websites to propagate his beliefs, without regard for the truth. Americans thought they had the right to peacefully protest, as a guarantee of our founding documents. He sends out his union buddies to hassle honest, hard working Americans who show up at public meetings to voice their opinions on major policy initiatives. (Can you imagine if Bush sent out his minions to confront liberal protesters?) President Obama cannot handle criticism and, at every chance he gets, he demonstrates his true beliefs and resorts to acting like a dictator. He truly believes he knows best. No one should question his policies.

No one need debate his policy initiatives. We should trust in him and one day we will wake up to the 'paradise' he has promised to deliver, whether we want his 'paradise' or not is irrelevant in his eyes. The man is a narcissist in the worst sense of that word.

Abolition of Religion. You thought you had freedom of religion. Well, if you are a Muslim or an atheist, okay, you still do. But if you practice any form of Judaea-Christian beliefs, your belief system will be mocked, disrespected, and hindered at every step. The Democrats have imposed a policy of separation of church and state that goes way beyond anything conceived by our founding fathers and have driven this concept to some of the most absurd practices.

Free Education. As stated by Marx and Engel, free public education is an important tenet of communism. The state needs to control education. These are the halls in which our children's minds are molded, not to be free thinkers but to be taught how to be good socialists. This is what our 'unionized' public school system is based on. They focus their teaching on political correctness and what a bad place America is, rather than teaching math and science. Recent gains by private charter schools are being challenged by the left and squashed at every corner as the unions refuse to allow a competitive educational environment in America. The real fear from charter schools is that they are proving themselves to be very effective at educating our children, even in the poorest urban communities. The charter schools are delivering higher test score rates, graduating a higher percentage of students, sending a higher percentage of students to college, and all of this for less cost per student than the public schools. The Democrats can't accept this. It destroys the need for teacher unions and demonstrates how ineffective the teacher unions have been in educating our children. The reason for this is simple: teacher unions care more about how much they can take from the educational system than on how to improve the educational value delivered to our children. I need to correct my statement that Democrats don't believe in charter schools. They do—but only for their own children. Starting with the President of the United States, and going down the congressional ranks, look at what schools their children go to.. Not the union controlled public school system, but elite, private institutions.

Were you aware that the Obama administration is essentially "nationalizing" colleges and post graduate institutions? Loans made by private companies to finance student loans are being abolished. All student loans will be made by our government.

Just one more instance of government taking control over every aspect of our lives. The ultimate goal will be become clear over the years to come. President Obama has already stated that he wants students to gravitate away from jobs he doesn't like—such as investment banking, financing, or anything else that has to do with Wall Street. Don't be shocked if in the future, our government tells the anxious student needing a loan to go to college that he/she can get government money but in exchange, they need to seek careers in certain pre-sanctioned industries or markets. Just one more step toward a socialist society.

In summary, a comparison of the core principles of Marx and Engel are very close to the core principles of our current President and the liberals in the Democratic Party. Health care reform, as presently proposed by our federal government, will provide the final transition from a capitalist America to a communist state. President Obama promised this in his campaign for President, carefully guarding his language to disguise what he truly seeks to accomplish. Only when he is off the teleprompter do you get clues as to how he really thinks. Speaker Pelosi and President Obama intend to deliver this no matter what the cost to the "Communist States of America!" Unfortunately, too many Republicans in our Congress, especially over the last decade, have been complicit by not speaking up and fighting the intrusion of government into our private lives. In fact, many Republicans have voted in support of the growing intrusion of our government, excessive spending, significants in regulatory actions, and the higher burden of taxes, fees and penalties on Americans. These Republicans are as responsible as the liberal Democrats in creating a socialist communist state.

CHAPTER FOUR

HOW DO WE SHAPE OUR ENERGY POLICY TO FURTHER THE ABILITY OF OUR COUNTRY TO MAINTAIN ITS ECONOMIC AND MILITARY SUPERIORITY?

Energy. The industrial revolution would not have occurred without it. The internet age cannot advance without it. The Internet is bringing the world closer together. And with that, trade is increasing. Nations that benefit off trade with each other rarely go to war. Global competition is good for the world. It will increase wealth and reduce poverty in many areas of the world. But if America wants to remain globally dominant then we must rely on no one but ourselves for our energy needs,.

The United States has sufficient natural gas and coal to power our economy for the next century, perhaps longer. We have enough oil to last us for decades. Our failure to utilize our natural resources is one of the biggest mistakes our government has made over the last three decades, and yet when this became obvious to us in the 1970's we did not heed the lessons but buried our heads in the sand. The solution to the energy problem is simple: become self reliant! The price of energy wil fall. Much of the current oil prices are based on the fact that the United States does not have the "will" to become self-reliant. Oil prices have dropped significantly since President Bush declared that we should drill our own oil, and they dropped even further due to our weak economy. Can you imagine if the idiots in Congress were to follow up on this situation with a real energy policy? Oil would more likely remain at reasonable prices for some time to come. The problem is that the Democrats don't want to lose this political issue and are therefore holding our economy, and the future wealth of America, hostage so as to appease the extreme left of their party and thus their political party's desire.

The fact is that the Democrats won the environmental war some time ago. Most Americans consider themselves to be environmentally friendly. Americans don't want to pollute or destroy the planet, but most Americans realize that energy can be obtained in environmentally friendly ways. Despite 'scare' reports, there is less than half a gallon of hydrocarbons leaking from oil platforms in the Gulf of Mexico. Americans leak more hydrocarbons from the gas tanks on their cars and boats each year than the massive platforms which deliver hundreds of thousands, if not millions, of gallons of oil each day to our markets.

Here is an energy policy that makes sense:

1. **Drill. On shore, off shore, oil shales. Drill anywhere oil can be found.** We have more untapped reserves of oil than Saudi Arabia. Why are we paying them and jeopardizing our economy? It is shameful that China can

drill off our own coasts but we can't. There is more oil in America than we can measure. It has been estimated that we have more oil than Saudi Arabia. The U.S. Dept of Interior estimates that we have 86 billion barrels of oil in the Outer Continental Shelf that is yet undiscovered, but fully recoverable. Industry experts believe this to be a very conservative estimate since the industry has been **PROHIBITED** by **CONGRESS** to explore this region for the last 26 YEARS. You've got to be kidding, right? But, according to our politicians, it is the fault of the oil companies that we have high oil prices! The technology to detect oil reserves today is far superior of where it was 26 years ago. Imagine how much oil is actually out there if we would allow our oil industry to look for it. This does not include what we have available in the midwest, Alaska, and other parts of this country. The next time you hear a politician rant about huge profits of the oil companies and proposing that something be done to stop them from raping the consumer, ask what percentage of sales the oil companies actually make in profits—the answer is under 10%. Then follow up with the question: "how much does the government take on leasing tracks of land in Alaska, the Gulf of Mexico, and the continental shelf to the oil companies?" The answer varies depending on the location but ranges between 37% and 51%, and, in some areas, even higher. Let's get this right: the US government has no risk, no investment, and no expenditure, yet it collects upwards of five times or more than the 'evil', 'unpatriotic' oil companies. Hmmm! If the government were serious about raising revenue, rather than higher taxes on the elements of our economy that produce, we should unleash our resources. For every barrel of oil we could produce in the United States, there is no segment of our economy that would benefit more then the coffers of our government. The Alaskan government was smart and drilled enough oil to enable them to pay thousands of dollars to every Alaskan citizen with their program to share the wealth of their natural resources. Perhaps our federal government could learn the lesson that leasing of federal property can be an enormous asset to lighten the burden to the US Taxpayer? Don't hold your breath. After taking a large share of the profits from oil companies, Congress places a hefty tax on gasoline so that every time we fill up our car, they get another piece of the pie.

2. **Build nuclear plants.** America has not built a nuclear plant in three decades. We have the "know-how" to build technologically safe nuclear plants. France has done this, and 80% of their energy is now produced by nuclear power. Not only should we emulate this, but imagine all the high paying jobs that would be created in the process. There is probably no more environmentally-safe manner in which to create energy for the next couple of decades. Nuclear power is one of the best green alternatives we have for energy. There is no carbon emission issue with nuclear power.

3. **Build oil refineries.** It has been decades since we have built new and additional oil refineries. There is no point

in drilling for more oil if we do not have the ability to refine the crude oil into useable forms of energy. If we can't refine the crude oil, we create a bottleneck for the delivery of oil to the consumer.

4. **Natural gas.** We have enormous natural gas supplies. This is a clean form of energy that already has a distribution system in place. We can safely power most of the products we use on a day-to-day basis with natural gas. The US Department of Interior estimates that we have 420 trillion cubic feet of natural gas yet undiscovered, but recoverable, from the Outer Continental Shelf.

5. **Coal.** Clean coal technology has made great strides. We need to create more energy plants that are powered by coal. Coal delivers inexpensive energy in great volumes. The U.S. has enormous volumes of coal resources—we are the Saudi Arabia of coal. Let's use it.

6. **Wind.** Wind farms are clean and renewable. America is, supposedly, also the Saudi Arabia of wind. We can build wind turbine farms throughout the plain states, and even offshore in many regions of the country, to deliver efficient and reasonably priced energy to communities across the country. Recent attempts, however, to build wind farms have been halted by the very environmentalists that are yelling at us for drilling oil and demand that we must use other forms of renewable energy: wind and solar. This is a sad joke that is strangling our renewable energy industry. Efforts to build a wind farm, whether off Ted Kennedy's Massachusetts or in California, just can't be done. Yet

China is planning to take the lead on wind farm power over the next few years while we sit immobile because of our environmentalists and politicians.

7. **Solar.** Like wind, the solar energy source has huge potential. Re-investment in technology will increase the efficiency of photo-voltaic cells. In the southern and western states, this is a source of energy that can, and should, become an important part of the overall energy profile. Recently, Governor Schwarzenneger has to build a solar energy complex in the Mojave Desert in southern California but with no luck. The environmental advocates won't allow it. If you can't build a solar farm in the desert, then where the heck can you build one? It is amazing to listen to our politicians decry that we must spend billions of our tax dollars to get off our addiction to oil, then when we offer a plan to do so, the same politicians say "No". We keep electing these morons; we have no one to blame but ourselves. The idea of green energy is great, even if it is more expensive, but we must build it.

8. **Hydrogen.** New power technologies will be released over the next few years for automobiles. Electric, solar, natural gas and hydrogen will be competing with oil as the power system for our vehicles. If electric powered vehicles gain popularity, our electric plant capacity must be increased to support the additional burden. Electric power plants are powered by nuclear, or coal, for the most part. Hydrogen is appealing, but the technology is not ready yet for mass acceptance. When hydrogen becomes economically

viable, the next challenge will be distribution. Hydrogen fueling stations will be needed at local gas stations to make it readily available, and convenient, to the consumer. We have the ability to produce hydrogen gas from bacteria that consumes our sewerage and other biomass products. We need to invest in this form of renewable energy. One thing we will always have plenty of, particularly in Washington D.C., is waste.

9. **Wave Energy.** This is a technology that is beginning to show promise in prototypes around the world. Portugal and Ireland are planning projects that will soon start producing energy for small communities. Waves are a constant source of energy, unlike wind or solar. Waves pound our shorelines incessantly and, since most of our population is along the coast lines of America, the production of this energy would not be far from the customers. Unfortunately, this is a renewable energy source that is much more expensive than oil (about ten times more expensive), but with larger projects coming on line, it is expected the costs will drop dramatically.

There are other sources of energy that we can tap into. Every local market needs to analyze what may work best, but in order to succeed our politicians must lead—something they rarely like to do because it opens them up to easy criticism. In some markets, energy from water might be the most ideal source, such as the power tapped from the Hoover Dam and Niagara Falls. Turbines under the ocean which take advantage of ocean currents could be another energy source in certain markets. Converting trash into energy has been done for decades, but our government has allowed this to become a political football. It is clean, renewable, and resolves the storage problem that every city in America has every day with its trash.

Our government needs to support, rather than prohibit, the race to find the most suitable and efficient sources of energy. Every level of government must make this a high priority. There must be a unified goal to find solutions enabling each community to be energy-independent within ten years. Do this one community at a time, across our nation, and this will happen. In this way, we can, and will be, energy independent. In fact, we have so many sources of energy available, we could sell our new technologies and excess energy to other nations of the world. This would put us into the position of being an energy exporter, raking in billions of dollars per year, to enrich our nation.

Note that corn ethanol was not included in the above plan. Production of corn ethanol requires more energy to create a gallon of fuel than if we were to just use oil. Currently the efficiency is not there to be a long term and sustainable supply. It also has the adverse effect of increasing food prices which the world cannot afford. Ethanol produced from sugar cane is considered a better alternative over corn ethanol. Brazil is an excellent example of this. They are much further along in establishing energy independence that we are.

CHAPTER FIVE
THE IMPORTANCE OF FREE TRADE

Free trade is good for America. It enriches nations and improves the lifestyle of citizens on both sides of the free trade fence. It has enabled democracies to prosper around the world. It has allowed peace to exist as the mainstay of foreign policy rather than war. Free trade tears down the walls that separate cultures and nations from one another. The old adage that nations with lots of McDonalds don't go to war with one another does have a ring of truth to it As nations trade with one another, the overall wealth of the citizens of each nation increases. As wealth increases, the wall of 'have nots' vs. 'haves' is lowered. A good example of this is Canada and the United States. We are great trading partners, stronger in recent decades than ever before. Mexico and the United States historically did very little trading. Canadians don't flood illegally into the United States because free trade has allowed the Canadian citizens to make money selling products (presently primarily natural resources) to the United States. Mexico, a poor country, had minimal trade with the United

States until the North American Free Trade Act (NAFTA) was passed. Since NAFTA, there has been a great increase in Mexico's trading with the United States. Mexico is progressing from a third world country to become a second world power. This takes time. The transformation is not something that can be measured over a few years, but over decades. As Mexico becomes a richer nation, it will produce sufficient jobs at home and its citizens will be able to support their families without traveling to the United States. Free trade with Mexico will help Mexico obtain that goal while at the same time, Mexico's buying power will result in the sale of more U.S. goods to Mexico, thus benefiting U.S. citizens in a direct way When the U.S. buys more products from Mexico, their citizens become enriched and the Mexicans will then buy more American cars, light bulbs, sodas, and so on. As sales of American products increase, American businesses will prosper and our citizens will have jobs at every level, from manager down to janitor. Mexico, however, must put an end to its corruption or the opportunity to have free trade improve their economy and lift the people out of poverty will not happen.

Why do we even debate the benefits of free trade in the United States? The answer is simple: our unions. Unions despise free trade because it causes a shift of jobs to foreign countries and, traditionally, those lost jobs had been the stronghold of unions. As pay scales skyrocketed in the United States, it became more economical to move those jobs to countries where costs of manufacturing, engineering, or development are cheaper. In other words, globalization. This means unions are losing the employees that pay the dues which support the union leaders.

This is a declining state of affairs for the unions. Therefore they can't afford to allow free trade to prevail, regardless that it benefits society overall. Accordingly, unions have huge reserves of funds they procure from union members' pay checks and they use those funds to promote political candidates who are sympathetic to the individual needs of the unions. This is contrary to the long term view that prosperity and peace will benefit the global community.

As an aside, the Obama administration is doing everything in its power to increase union membership in the United States. Congress is considering bills to allow unions to organize private companies by changing rules that have been in place since 1934. Some of the legislation being considered include, doing away with the secret ballot in union elections, changing rules of the election so that only 50% of those employees who want a union need to vote in favor of the union to require the private company to unionize, or forcing private companies who do business with the government to unionize (or agree to pay union dues on any contract with the government). All of this will lead to unions increasing union membership from approximately 8% of the labor force in private companies to something many times that number. The result, a huge drain on the American economy, making it more difficult for America to compete effectively with China, Brazil, India, Europe and so on. It is American productivity that currently keeps America as the leading economy in the world. Private companies are many times more productive than unionized companies. Socialist politics, however, has no care for global economic competitiveness, productivity of workers or technology gains. Trade between nations increases the wealth of all parties involved but we must have an economic advantage to maximize our international trade opportunities. Socialism doesn't care much about international trade either.

Evidence of how the Obama administration may harm to the American economy, the average middle-class worker, is Canada. Fearful of Obama's administration, Canada announced it was meeting with the President of France in an effort to increase shipments of goods and trade to France and Europe on free trade principles that are more generous than the free trade premises of NAFTA. Canada has already announced that Obama's stated intention of unilaterally renegotiating NAFTA is off limits to our northern friends. Thus, they will reduce trade with the United States and increase trade with Europe. Who loses? The United States worker loses. Be prepared. In every facet of the health of our economy, our current Congress will destroy decades of success and growth that had kept America the premier economy in the world. They are already having their impact by making our current economic woes worse than they otherwise need to be.

CHAPTER SIX

WHAT MUST WE DO FROM A NATIONAL SECURITY PERSPECTIVE TO MAXIMIZE THE SAFETY OF SECURITY OF OUR COUNTRY AND WHAT ROLE OUR MILITARY MUST PLAY TO ASSIST IN ACHIEVING THIS GOAL?

President George W. Bush was right. In order to protect America we need to be on the offense, not the defense. We must treat those who want to harm America as a wartime enemy. We will not succeed in protecting our country if we return to the days of treating terrorists as criminals, rather than as warriors. Our state, local and federal police agencies are certainly a part of the overall security mechanism acting as an umbrella protecting our country, but we need the efforts of our military, national intelligence, and special operations units, to bring the war to the enemies. Since 9/11, President Bush has been successful in obviating potential attacks on our country. No attack occurred in the time frame after 9/11 through the end of his administration. Frankly, that is a remarkable record when one considers the openness of American society and the ease with which so many illegal immigrants pass through our porous borders.

Future presidents should heed the lessons learned during the Bush administration and build upon its successes. Our security apparatus must be ever vigilant and must continuously test its system for any weakness that our enemies can penetrate. Our security system must seek to peer into the future and evaluate the varying possibilities and probabilities of new forms and methods of attacks. Our enemies are constantly dreaming up new and improved ways to destroy us and we need to stay a step ahead. We must establish levels of infiltration within the heart of our enemies operations. Human capital cannot be substituted. We need to recruit and expand our human intelligence. Nothing replaces feet on the ground. We must use every form of electronic surveillance currently available to augment the resources of our human assets.

Our success on the military front is critical to maintaining our economic super power status. If we lose the war on terror, issues relating to our economy, health care, educating our children, and such other social issues that, indeed, are important to us, just won't matter. We will have much bigger problems to deal with, like survival and freedom.

In the early months of the Obama administration, it became clear on just how quickly the security of our nation can be impacted by bad decisions. It is apparent this administration is hostile toward the American military and any superior power it projects throughout the world. Obama apologizes for this at every opportunity. The decision to close Guantanamo Bay originated on political correctness, rather than protecting our security interests. Placing Leon Panetta in charge of our CIA indicates to the world that our intelligence agency has succumbed to political interests over national security interests. Limiting eavesdropping capabilities of our intelligence agency in the interest of political imaging will hinder our ability to detect enemy plans in a timely manner. Unilateral nuclear disarmament will prove to be a big mistake. Slowing down, or eliminating, our missile defense systems will prove itself an even larger mistake. This administration has already made significant cuts in the budget of the defense department and has suggested more is to come. Some defense projects deserve to be cut. It has not been unusual for projects to be kept active solely because the jobs relative to the project are located in an important congressional district and this supersedes the value the defense project may have to our nation's security. These decisions should be made by our military brass, outside the political influence of congressmen.

The Obama administration, led by Speaker Pelosi, is damaging the ability of the C.I.A. to recover the intelligence it needs in order to secure our country from future threats. Our current administration and the leaders of Congress harass the CIA on practically a daily basis. The next time a crisis occurs, these same politicians who are now impeding the capability of the CIA to perform its tasks, will likely complain about how ineffective the CIA is. National security should not be treated as a ping pong ball that gets slapped back and forth across the table depending on short term political winds.

On a positive note, President Obama's foreign policy looks very similar to that of President Bush. Keeping Robert Gates as Secretary of Defense was a good choice. He is continuing, and even accelerating, the fight against the Taliban in Afghanistan. He is allowing continued use of our drones to drop bombs on terrorist hide outs. However, the President's indecisiveness respecting whether to follow the advice of his generals and add more troops to Afghanistan is sending the wrong message to world leaders. I fear that his waffling on such a major decision will result in nation's throughout the world coming to one understanding: President Obama's administration can be pushed around. He talks a good game but never follows through on decisive action. This is not a good reputation to build in international affairs, and will likely come back to create trouble for the US in the future.

One of my largest concerns over the direction of the Obama administration is his naiveté with nations like Iran. While he is waiting for Iran to "please, oh please meet with me", Iran is perhaps only a few months away from being able to build a nuclear weapon. It is possible that Iran will meet with the U.S. and play the game with the UN solely as a tactic to stall Israel from taking any action in their hope of a diplomatic breakthrough. Yet every day that goes by, Iran is a day closer to having the ability to eliminate the state of Israel, destabilize the Mideast, and perhaps force an 'Armageddon like situation.' This administration's inability to lead by strength will open doors for those who want to harm us. My prediction: Iran will talk peace until it has built up adequate air power defenses to fend against an Israeli air strike, then Iran will break negotiations and do as it pleases.

CHAPTER SEVEN
WHY OUR CHILDREN MUST GET A WORLD CLASS EDUCATION

Our children are our future. We cannot have a successful society unless we take the time and investment to properly educate our children. This goes back to ensuring our economy remains globally competitive and at the top of its game. It cannot do this if we fail to educate our children in a way that develops our children into the best scientists, smartest business managers, best teachers, most competent professionals, etc., in the world. Our educational system is broken and has caused a decline in the performance of our students when matched against most of our industrial competitors.

We have spent enormous sums of money toward the goal of creating a world class education system. As a matter of fact, we spend more money per student than most other countries, yet we are not producing the smartest students in the world. Our education system is at the bottom of industrialized nations. We should be ashamed of ourselves. Why? There is a lot of blame to go around.

Here is s summary of some of the issues we face:

Tenure for teachers does not create a system that keeps our teachers at the top of their profession. Like every other worker in our society, our teachers need to be accountable for their performance in the classroom. There is no tenure in business,. Every day is a new day and, if you fail to perform, you lose your job. This may be draconian, but it is a huge incentive to encourage performance at the highest levels. Incentives are good. Teachers should be compensated based on how well they perform their tasks which should be measured by the performance of their students. Our current system on paying teachers based on tenure does nothing to promote a better education program. (This will be discussed in more detail.)

Students are pandered by their parents more so than ever before and appear to have lost their drive to work hard. In fact, most students seem to "expect" things to be given to them, rather than their having to spend years earning them. Employers are constantly complaining that young workers start new careers with lists of things they won't do on the job, such as coming to work early, staying late, working weekends, doing jobs that are 'beneath' them, etc. When I started working I never would have told any employer that any aspect of the job was unacceptable. I was just happy that someone would pay me. To this day, I will do whatever it takes, and work whatever hours are necessary, to adequately perform my job. I still work early mornings, late nights and even weekends pursuing a career of over twenty-eight years. This is what it takes to be successful. Students today have learned how to use our system to encourage laziness and just 'get by.'

An inherent problem of our education system is that there is no competition. Our public school system has a monopoly on educating our children. Most of them do a poor job of it. Competition always offers better options. If we are serious about educating our children, we would demand options in education. The old adage, "the cream will rise to the top" is still true. Private schools are often a good option here. Students in private schools tend to outperform those students who are enrolled in the public school system. Our government, if it were serious about improving education in America, as opposed to promoting teachers unions, would welcome, and promote, competition in the educational system. Our government should provide parents with tax credits if they choose to send their children to private schools. In this environment, parents will vote with their dollars. In poor community's as much as middle class communities, parents will push their educators to improve the education system. Public schools will need to compete for students or risk losing students to private schools. Private schools will seek to provide a better quality education at lower prices in an effort to increase their own student population. The end result, the students win, which means we all win. They will get a better quality education in both public and private schools as each sector of the educational system strives to compete for the same students.

Assuming we can bring competition to the education system, than why not reward our best teachers with market oriented incentives? Why not treat our teachers like we treat our managers? We make demands. We set goals. We mandate certain minimum performance criteria. And, when the individual teacher meets these goals, they get a monetary bonus. If they exceed the goals, they get a bigger bonus. In fact, the higher the performance, the higher the pay. Incentivize our teachers to be the best. Teachers that want to excel should have a compensation package rewarding their excellence. Of course, unions won't like this because they seek to rate everyone at the same level. Those who excel must be pulled down to the level of those who wish to be mediocre. Education will never reach the levels we know are possible if we don't motivate people who want to enter a teaching career and reward them when they deliver excellent results. The key word here is, of course, "deliver". Their earning capacity is tied to their performance. Sounds like the world most of live in; it can work in our education system.

We also need to re-evaluate what it is our students are being taught in our schools. Today, the curriculum has been curved to allow students to get through the system without learning to read well, write well, perform simple math, and understand world geography. We have a federal department of education that was established to set minimum standards for education and ANY student who cannot meet these minimum criteria does not graduate. Our students need to be proficient at math, science, reading, and writing. Our students should know geography, understand world events, comprehend our nation's history, and have a grasp on world history. We need to train our students to be world leaders, great scientists, top business leaders, or the best at whatever career choice they ultimately choose. We also need to look to the future and establish a core curriculum that will put our children at a maximum advantage in preparation for future careers. For example, we know that high technology, biotech, and life sciences will be important growth industries driving the American economy in the future. Accordingly, our school curriculum needs to put greater emphasis on math, sciences, computer and technology related courses. Our children need to be able to compete with students from around the world, many of whom are already ahead of the United States in the education of their children in these core curriculums.

Federal grants given to state educational systems can mandate certain advancements in technological curriculum in order to nurture the seeds necessary to teach our children skills they will need to succeed in their future. More emphasis needs to be placed on ensuring our children learn math and science. Incentives can be given to teachers for raising the educational skill set of their students above national levels. Schools have to be able to terminate teachers who are underperforming. The status quo is not acceptable and should not be tolerated.

Remember, our government is inept. We cannot allow our government to run our schools, (or healthcare). Everything government touches is badly mismanaged and costs many times what it should to deliver the same level of services from a private provider. You need to get involved with your local school boards and call for action to improve education. This is not done by throwing more dollars down the cesspool of government financing, but through economic incentives and increased competition that will do the heavy lifting of improvements, ultimately for the benefit for all of us. You need to know who is sitting on your local school boards. These individuals have enormous impact on your children and few of us have any clue as to who is running our schools and what decisions are being made. As a parent, we spend more time thinking about how to get our kids into the fall soccer program or spring baseball team than we do paying attention to the educational value being delivered in our local schools.

CHAPTER EIGHT
HOW SOCIAL SECURITY HAS SUCKED THE WEALTH OUT OF OUR SENIOR CITIZENS AND CAUSED THEM TO BE DEPENDENT ON GOVERNMENT RATHER THAN INDEPENDENT.

Our politicians have been so successful in scaring Americans about social security that it has become a topic that does not allow for intelligent debate on how to fix the broken system. Social Security is in a downward spiral toward insolvency. Yet, at the same time, our Social Security system has deprived Americans of a financially secure retirement. For each dollar Americans privately invest (whether in real estate, stocks, art, classic cares, fine wines, etc.), over time these investments tend to increase in value at rates that enrich the investors. With social security, for every dollar the government appropriates from your pay every pay period, the probability is that you will see either no rate of return on your investment or a very small rate of return significantly below market rates of return. In fact, if you die prematurely, there is no 'real' asset to pass onto to your family except some fractional monthly payment the government chooses to bestow onto your spouse. The system is in need of radical change. If one puts money in an IRA, they get a reasonable rate of return. There is little, or no, rate of return from our government and they pay back pennies in return for the money they seize which they have had the benefit of using for up to forty years or more. This has become even truer with our younger workers.

The system is broken. Social Security accounts for 23% of federal spending. It is the largest and most expensive retirement system in the world. Approximately 80% of Americans pay more social security taxes than federal taxes. Beginning in 2018, Social Security will be paying out more money to retirees than it will be taking in. As a result, every year past 2018, Social Security will be running a deficit. Choices need to be made. Either significant tax increases to pay for the deficits, or cuts in benefits, are the top resolutions discussed whenever the social security debate occurs. Many of our politicians rely on the same old answer—tax more. By the way, current projections are that social security taxes will need to double in order to keep Social Security in the black in coming decades.

Other solutions include making hard choices, like raising the retirement age with the argument that people are living longer, although, if healthcare reform is passed as currently proposed by the liberals in Congress, this may no longer be the trend. Others say we need both tax increases and benefit cuts. Projections suggest that taxpayers will have to fund hundreds of billions of dollars each year to fund Social Security deficits. This is a significant and worrisome amount of money on top of the trillions of dollars of additional expenditures already committed to by the Obama administration. Where is all this money going to come from? Where else but the taxpayer? But that begs the question: how much higher a tax burden can our workers afford before the whole system collapses under the weight of socialism?

We can come up with smarter and better long term fixes. Our government needs to provide us with more options. One option is to allow our citizens to privately invest for their own retirement as an alternative to giving it to the government, subject to strict regulatory schemes, so that the retirement capital cannot be invested in speculative investments. Raising taxes to solidify the foundation of social security is not a solution. Cutting social security benefits is suicide for any politician. The only solution is to give the individual some control over their own retirement account. This will provide the worker with more flexibility in saving for his/her retirement. It will provide the worker with a positive rate of return, as opposed to little, or no, rate of return. In turn, it will provide the worker with a higher quality of life upon retiring.

Currently, it is estimated that a 25 year old will pay more money into social security then he/she will ever collect. That is correct, a negative rate of return. Clearly, the 25 year old is better off having control over his/her retirement dollars and, even in the most conservative portfolio, over their working lifetime, will have a significant positive rate of return. If we are trying to mandate savings for retirement so that future generations of senior citizens have a nest egg with which to retire on, then government control of our retirement dollars is not the answer. Any solution to Social Security must seek to attain a nest egg that grows in value over and above the amount invested by the worker out of his/her payroll earnings. In order to accomplish this goal, the social security system must permit individuals to have control over how their retirement dollars are invested. The government will need to regulate these personal retirement accounts closely and limit the investment options a person can choose, so as to ensure the retirement dollars are conservatively invested and not gambled on speculative and risky ventures. Nonetheless, this is the only long term solution that makes economic sense for our country, provides the worker with a reasonable rate of return on dollars invested, provides higher quality of life upon retirement, and does not increase the tax burden on American workers. It is a win-win for all involved.

CHAPTER NINE
BACK TO THE ECONOMY—
THE TRUTH BEHIND WHO CAUSED
THE 2008 FINANCIAL CRISIS

Wall Street imploded in the fourth quarter of 2008 and first quarter of 2009. The political pundits blame Wall Street greed and talked about the need for greater regulation to curb their greed. Let's put things in perspective. This problem started with the Community Reinvestment Act passed during the Jimmy Carter administration. The purpose of this Act was to create the American dream of home ownership to lower middle class and poor families of America. It was a noble cause indeed. During the Clinton Administration, and even during the early years of the Bush administration, this program grew to create the Fannie Mae and Freddie Mac monsters.

Wall Street and American banks were forced to substantially increase lending to those in our society that were less creditworthy. In the end, all of this cheap money emanated, through greed, to all segments of our society. Speculators got involved. Real Estate developers followed. Middle America got on the train also. Greed did enter the market, but greed is good. Greed is what built this country into the strongest and richest country the world has ever seen. If we got rid of greed and adopted socialist policies, then we must recognize that the economic engine that got us here will not continue to keep us #1. Perhaps that is okay for many who enjoy being dependent of the government to provide their needs and lifestyle. I prefer to be responsible for my own lifestyle. That is not saying that I believe there should be no safety net, I do, and a strong one at that. Government has a role to play, but the government never accepts that often times they makes things worse, rather than better. The government is inefficient. They are blow hards. They whine. They fail to recognize that the best leaders lead, and do not follow the daily whims of polls. They spend way too much money. They take too much money from the people. They enrich themselves with retirement plans, health benefits, trips around the world, etc., that the rest of us can only dream about. They complain about the amount of money earned by executives, yet they live like royalty on the public dole. They complain about the private sector using private aircraft, yet Congress recently just spent half a billion dollars of our tax dollars on private jets for our royal congressional representatives. Obama uses Air Force One to take his wife on date nights. They are hypocrites! They get paid large sums of money to talk nonsense, and most times they do nothing. When they do finally do something, it is usually the wrong thing.

What was the real cause of the economic meltdown of our financial services industry and the subprime crisis? Politicians have blamed the mortgage brokers and banks for having made bad loans. This is true. Our financial system should never have allowed people to buy homes with little, and even no, money down. Loans were granted without any loan documentation. Loans were issued to people with no due diligence of their individual financial wherewithal to repay. How could we have been so stupid? Why would we as a nation embark on such a weak foundation without realizing that the inevitable result would have to be an implosion of this market?

The answer may surprise you. The answer lies at the feet of Congress. You will not hear our politicians tell us the trouble started with them. The news media won't tell you, either, because they have their own agenda. Step back in time. Fannie Mae and Freddie Mac were originally established to promote loans to low-income people so they could buy houses and be owners in the American dream. No one can deny that this goal was a nice idea. The problem is that too many of these people could not afford to come up with the customary down payment and could not meet the requirement of traditional lending standards. As a result, the Federal Reserve, particularly under Alan Greenspan and during the Clinton administration, pumped enormous liquidity into the financial services industry in order to give loans to people that could not afford them. They offered mortgage plans designed to allow people at the bottom half of our economic ladder to obtain home ownership. Congress had put into motion the very seeds that caused the current real estate bubble. The mortgage brokers and banks are not to be blamed for taking the money that was thrown their way for them to lend—that is what they get paid

Back to the Economy...

to do. That is what they were told to do. They supported their families and built their own financial wealth by doing so. And thus, the real estate boom was born. Supply and demand worked. Builders built and people bought. Values went up because the demand to buy was greater than the supply of real estate. New development it was being sold out over a weekend. Everyone was happy. Everyone was making money. Home ownership among the lowest income classes skyrocketed. The leaders of Fannie Mae and Freddie Mac were buoyed by Congress for doing such a wonderful job and the politicians chose their closest friends, (all Democrats by the way), to lead these organizations and reward them with bonuses totaling tens of millions of dollars. Franklin Raines headed up Fannie Mae and collected $100 million in bonuses. That was okay because Mr. Raines was a close friend with politicians like Barney Frank. Fannie Mae did more to create the real estate bubble than anyone else, except for our Congress. President George W. Bush went to Congress 17 times during his administration to decry that the system was broken and needed repair. No one in Congress would listen, especially people like Barney Frank and Chris Dodd. Bubbles are fun on the way up, but a nightmare when they pop and come down. It is ironic that President Bush got blamed for an economic implosion that actually resulted from the real estate bubble that the Democrats had created.

The Enron crisis was another problem. What did the implosion of Enron have to do with our current financial crisis? It has a great deal to do with it. When Enron imploded, our politicians reacted the typical way they do when any crisis occurs.

They all got together, found someone to blame, and then "fixed" the problem so it "can never happen again" (how many times have we heard this?). In other words, they pass reform legislation with even more regulation. When the Enron crisis occurred, Congress reacted by enacting a new law, called the Sarbanes-Oxley Act. This Act added many new financial controls and, specifically, accounting treatment of how U.S. businesses govern themselves. The Act also sought to make senior management of U.S. business accountable imposing large fines and criminal penalties. This has prompted many new companies to leave our country and go to places, like London, to raise capital. This Act caused New York City to lose its status as the #1 financial market in the world. Business leaders thrive on taking risks and then hope that the risks they've taken work in the marketplace. If the results of the risks fail to occur as planned, the last thing they need is criminal prosecution just because some second guessing bureaucrat, who has no comprehension of the business world, seeks to put them in jail just to make a name for themselves.

Another thing this Act did was to pass a regulation requiring businesses to "mark their assets to market". In summary, this little jewel has had an enormous role to play in our financial mess of 2008. It was a critical component of the financial mess created by Fannie Mae and Freddie Mac by becoming a financial typhoon that rocked the very foundation of some of our largest and strongest financial institutions.

Let me give you a real world example. A commercial bank has a real estate loan to a borrower that, at time of the loan closing, appeared to be a strong loan based on significant due diligence, reasonable risks, and traditional loan documentation supporting the risk the bank was taking. The loan closed in 2006. Then, in late 2008, the subprime crisis caused deflation of real estate values, chased away buyers, and created fear that the bursting of the real estate bubble would take a long time to recover. In this example, our borrower never missed a monthly payment. The borrower was still performing from a monetary standpoint and making his monthly mortgage payments on a timely basis. Nonetheless, the "mark to market" rule of Sarbanes-Oxley requires the commercial bank to re-value the real estate. The property is no longer worth what it was at time of closing in 2006 and has dropped in value. The bank has no choice but to write down the value of the asset to its value in 2008. As a result, the bank contacts the borrower and tells him he has to come up with a sizeable down payment because the loan-to-value ratio is not consistent with the original covenants of the loan agreement. The borrower has no way to come up with any additional down payment. The bank is now forced to treat this performing loan, at least in regard to the monthly payments are concerned, as a non-performing loan. The current regulations require the bank place a 'loan loss reserve' on its books in order to recognize the risk that this loan may not be repaid. This means that the bank has to reduce its net capital by the amount of the 'loan loss reserve.' By taking "dollars" from its net capital account into its loan loss reserve account, the bank loses the ability to "lend" that net capital back into the market. Banks make money from lending.

The economy grows when the input of capital into the economy gives businesses growth capital in order to increase their businesses, expand jobs, build plants, etc. Imagine the above scenario happens with, not one or two borrowers, but in every bank in the country with a sizeable percentage of their loans. The result is a full-fledged liquidity crisis. Banks no longer have any capital to lend. When banks stop lending, the engine of economic growth seizes and the downward spiral begins. Unfortunately, most of the loans being placed into 'loan loss reserves' are not uncollectible or bad loans. Most of these losses will become nothing more than paper losses that, as the markets turn, will revert back into assets. In the meantime, we are caught in a serious financial crunch that can trigger a global depression.

If you have been paying attention during the latest meltdown on Wall Street, you heard from politicians across our country that the reason we are in this mess is because there has been too much deregulation. I laugh at that. So should you. Deregulation is not the culprit. Poor regulation in the past is the root cause of the financial crisis of 2008. Bad regulation includes forcing our financial industry to give loans to people that were not creditworthy, and causing our banking system to seize from the "mark to market" regulation.

There is a solution, and it is not more regulation. We need to create liquidity in the capital markets and get our banks back into the business of lending. To do this, we must free up the capital currently tied up as paper losses on the balance sheets of our banks. One solution being discussed is to have a government created Resolution Trust Company purchase all the 'bad' loans from the banks. We need to remove these toxic assets from our system but, even more crucial, is to allow the banks to handle their own loan portfolio. They are more familiar with their bad loans than any bureaucrat ever will. Let's give our bankers the tools they need to sort out and manage their own bad loans while at the same time we pump more capital liquidity into the banking system so they can continue to lend money into our economy. Any solution that ignores the need to provide liquidity for the capital markets will not produce the optimal results desired.

The solution proposed by the Democrats will only serve to substantially weaken the economy. Their program of imposing higher taxes, additional government regulation, more class warfare, more socialism, and derailment of free trade policies will only accelerate and prolong the decline of the U.S. economy. Obama proudly asserts that he will reduce taxes for 95% of Americans and that only the rich in America will pay additional taxes. Let's cut through this double-talk. First of all: 40% of Americans don't even pay taxes, so how does he cut taxes on 95% of Americans? You can't cut taxes for people who do not even pay taxes. This means, in real terms, that Americans who work, Americans who create jobs, Americans who take risks to invest capital in hopes of getting a greater return, and Americans who accept risks of their livelihood in hopes of acquiring a piece of the American dream, will be punished in a social redistribution program. The democrat program will take from those that produce, and give to those who do not produce. How can any American think this is good policy? How can they expect this policy to translate into a stronger, richer nation able to compete against China, Russia, India, and even Brazil, and Ireland?

To put things in perspective, the U.S. economy in the years George W. Bush had been President grew by approximately 19%. This is about 50% to 70% faster than our European counterparts and yet the liberals in our country are desperate to emulate them. Japan only grew 13% during the Bush years. Our economy will recover under the direction of Obama; not because of his policies, but despite them. However, the increase in economic growth will be less and the time needed to recover will be longer. You can expect, though, that the media, which is strongly biased, will hail his recovery as miraculous even though it will pale to the economic environment Ronald Reagan and George W. Bush gave us. The basic reason Obama's recovery will not be as strong as past recoveries goes back to lessons learned in basic economics compounded with Obama's plan to redistribute wealth. When 1% of the population pays an extraordinarily large share of all the taxes in the U.S., any attempt to squeeze more of the tax burden from these few productive workers will, at some point, negatively affect economic growth. Where does it stop? Should the top 1% of Americans pay 100% of the taxes for the rest of us? Would this be fair? Obama clearly thinks it is. Currently, the top 1% pay more in taxes than the bottom 95% of all taxes in America. Obama clearly intends to make this even worse. He proposes that the top 1% should pay for healthcare for the rest of America. The top 1% should pay for other Americans to have new, fuel-efficient cars. The top 1% should pay for retirement benefits for all Americans. The top 1% should provide housing subsidies to the rest of the Americans. It won't be long before we won't have a top 1% to pay for stuff

Back to the Economy...

for the rest of us. The top 1% (and the 5% immediately below them) will either leave the country, or at least move their wealth outside the country; or they will stop creating wealth because it no longer benefits them. Either case will destroy the long-term prospects of the American economy, and the American dream with it. This will impair our ability to be globally competitive and the leading economic engine of the world.

Do you want proof? Look at California. Governor Schwarzenegger said California had taxed the rich so heavily in their state, that the rich are leaving the state in droves. Over the last two years, hundreds of thousands of people have left California and relocated in states with less taxes and regulatory restraints. Even the poor are leaving the state of California as they realize that the jobs, and job growth, is no longer in California, but in neighboring states. Californians are notorious for embracing liberal policy ideas, but the reality of economics is now hitting hard. With the top 1% of California's population paying over 50% of California's tax burden, the scales have tipped, and the population is voicing their vote with their feet - by leaving the state. America, under Obama, is following the same path.

There is a solution: tie the hands of our politicians with constitutional amendments at state and federal levels to prohibit the government from spending progressively more money each year by limiting the increase of government spending to inflation, plus factoring in population growth or decline, unless approved by a referendum vote of 60% or greater.

CHAPTER TEN
IMMIGRATION MUST BE SOLVED

Immigration is a critical issue for the growth of our country. Our immigration policy is broken. One of the key components to the success of America over the last two hundred years has been our ability to take some of the best and brightest people from countries all over the world to come to America, make it their home, and devote their hard work, energy, loyalty, blood and capital into making this the greatest country the world has ever seen.

Our current policy is puzzling because it creates enormous obstacles blocking the best and brightest from contributing to America. The world has looked upon America as the land of opportunity and, as a result, the world's population arrived in droves to help build our country. Nowadays we chase our brightest foreign students and foreign workers out of the United States. This is just stupid. Many foreigners in America don't need government support. They work hard, own real estate, operate businesses and contribute to the economic well being of our country every day. It is just senseless that we force these people out of our country.

We need tight border control to prevent criminals and terrorists from entering our country. This is a matter of enforcement and it should be strict. But the price of securing our borders should not exclude talented, hard working families from coming to America and staying here as long as they want—hopefully forever. Any foreigner who has no red flags in their personal history and who is educated, owns real estate, businesses, or works regularly at businesses in America, should be able to stay in our country. The sign at our border should say: "If you have real skills, or assets sufficient to support yourself, then we want you, now and forever."

The visa process should promote this process rather than being an obstacle to their contribution to our country. Let them pay taxes. Let them pay for education. Let them pay for healthcare. But also let them work and live in a free country that accepts diversity, incentivizes opportunity, and cherishes their hard work and loyalty to our country. At the same time, double our investment to stop bad people from entering our country.

It is more worrisome that America is beginning to suffer a brain drain. Some of the brightest and most talented Americans are now leaving the U.S. and going elsewhere. An astonishing 40% of science and engineering PhD's awarded by American universities are to foreign students. We need these individuals to stay here. It is their brainpower that can help propel America to new heights in coming decades. It is beyond foolish to let this talent leave our shores. Our immigration policy needs to be reformed to make the process of keeping such talent much simpler and more efficient. America will not prosper, and will not remain competitive in the next century, without retaining this vast source of brainpower.

In addition, Americans themselves are seeking opportunities overseas because America is losing its position as the land of opportunity. This flight of intellectual capital from America will have long-term adverse consequences for the health of our economy. The more socialist that our country becomes, the more that Americans will leave our borders. Entrepreneurs can work in any environment and they will establish their business under economic conditions that are favorable to their business. Our scientists and financial geniuses can also work anywhere in the world. Our bright professionals are in great demand by rising world economies. Our rich have the ability to live anywhere. The current atmosphere in Washington DC is prompting our best to leave America, and I predict this process will accelerate. Talk to your neighbors and you will discover that people are leaving, applying for dual citizenship with other countries. Americans are resilient. They will find a means to apply their skills and reap rewards for their hard work; if not here, then elsewhere.

Our country should not only embrace immigration, we should welcome emigration. We should support those Americans who don't like our country and wish to leave. We should send people who believe America is the problem in the world to any country they think is better. In fact, this program could be the best stimulus for our economy. Instead of spending $780 billion dollars on 'pork' projects that will have no actual effect to stimulating the U.S. economy, we should take that money and give it to the Liberals if they leave our country. It would be less expensive to ship Liberals back to Europe than to keep them here and allow them to seize our wealth. Provide them a one-way plane ticket, buy their existing home, and even offer to subsidize their income for a few months while they re-establish themselves in the foreign country of their choice. The houses acquired from the Liberals being emigrated can be sold to foreigners who want to enter America, be a part of the American dream and assist America in our effort to be the greatest country the world has ever known.

Substituting American haters with hard working people that see America as the great opportunity she is, will stimulate our economy to new heights and stop the economic disaster Liberals are creating at home. Additionally, Liberals can go to countries that actually need their help. In Venezuela they will be welcomed as heroes. The Liberals can be at peace knowing they live in a country that think like they do. They can help Chavez nationalize any industry he has not yet taken over. ACORN can follow the Liberals to Venezuela for they can assist in making sure that Chavez is always re-elected with 100% of the vote. If Venezuela is not enough of a challenge, they could also go to Iran, Syria, Lebanon or Palestine to teach Muslims how to be peace-loving people who should not be trying to take over the world with their radical Islam precepts. There is a lot of work that can be done in these countries. Who better than an American liberal to spread the liberal word around the world as a missionary of peace? If we could get American liberals to do this, they would actually be serving America in a positive way. They want to change the world and I think they should be allowed to do so. Let's help them by sending them out from our shores. Taxes should go to building a stronger America by paying for a strong emigration program.

CHAPTER ELEVEN
HEALTHCARE

The U.S. Post Office
Department of Motor Vehicles
Social Security Administration
Medicare
Medicaid
Veterans Affairs Administration
Department of Elections
Department of Education
Environmental Protection Agency

I rest my case. Is there a government department, agency, or authority that you know of that is well managed and cost effective? I can't think of one at any level of government. Now the Obama administration suggests we should trust our health care to government bureaucrats. If you don't like your doctor, you can change. With government overseeing healthcare, a commission of bureaucrats will decide on what care you get, what pill you

Healthcare

take, and how many days, weeks or months you must wait to get care. It is unbelievable that anyone would consider changing the best healthcare system in the world to have healthcare doled out to us by Department of Motor Vehicle type bureaucrats—and it will cost more to boot. Have we lost our minds?

Nothing More Needs to Be Said.

CHAPTER TWELVE
HEALTHCARE REFORM—
WHAT THIS IS REALLY ALL ABOUT

I wish I could leave the healthcare argument with only the small paragraph written in the previous Chapter but, unfortunately, (or fortunately?), I believe that Americans need to hear the facts about healthcare reform as proposed by Liberals. There are also some common sense solutions that can help solve the problem.

First, let's discuss what Liberals are up to.

The dirty little secret about health care reform really has little to do with improving healthcare in America. In fact, healthcare reform as envisioned by Congress will reduce the quality of care, substantially increase the costs, and dramatically ration care, especially for the elderly. Healthcare reform is all about the core principles of progressive politics in America. They are offering power in the government rather than power to the people. That is what this is all about. Liberals do not trust individuals to make decisions for themselves. Liberals do not believe in individual freedom. Liberals do not believe in liberty. The fact that America was founded on the core principles of individual liberty and freedom means nothing to Liberals. Liberals believe in the 'nanny state' run by liberal bureaucrats who tell everyone else what to do.

Of course, Liberals cannot tell Americans the truth of what they seek for Americans will reject it out of hand. Therefore, Liberals disguise their desire for a 'nanny state' by creating disingenuous arguments about the moral obligation to help 47 million people who are uninsured, and how struggling American families have a "right" to "free" healthcare and, of course, these lofty goals can be achieved without enlarging the national deficit. We will examine the falsehood behind the Liberal arguments later in this chapter but first, heed this warning: If Liberals are successful in establishing the type of healthcare reform they have been campaigning on for the last several decades, then America, as a nation, will have its brightest days behind it. Health care reform will either create massive deficits, ala what Medicare and Medicaid have already caused, or the tax burden on the American worker will so greatly increase that it will choke the American economic engine that, for the average person, has catapulted us to be the richest, most generous, nation in the world.

President Obama, on July 22, 2009, in his press conference on healthcare reform, stated that Medicare and Medicaid are going broke. Not breaking news. We all know this. His solution is not to find a way to fix these broken programs that are bankrupting the nation. Instead, his solution will make the problem bigger by insisting on a national healthcare program which is nothing more than extending Medicare and Medicaid to every citizen. His resolution will maintain these failed programs by supporting them with huge new tax increases placed on the backs of all taxpaying Americans. His solution is to tax small businesses to the point where they can no longer compete, must cease hiring new employees, or go out of business altogether. Medicare and Medicaid have an estimated $70-$120 billion, or more, in fraud each year. This would be a good place to start in solving our healthcare problems, instead of creating a massive new, additional, program that will undoubtedly result in a bloated bureaucracy and billions of dollars per year in new fraud.

Healthcare costs have increased substantially over the past few decades and mechanisms to control these costs must be considered. The reason healthcare costs have increased is not due to a conspiracy by drug companies or insurance companies, as advocated by the Liberals. Healthcare costs have skyrocketed for many reasons. one of with the most instrumental is that our population is aging and, without argument, old people need more healthcare than young people. The bulk of healthcare costs are spent during the last 6 months of one's life. This is not a surprising fact. Also, the advantage of having the highest technology, along with the best drugs, costs considerable money. This is one of the primary reasons people from all over the world come to America for healthcare. We have the best. The best costs money.

To control healthcare costs the answer is not more regulation; that only serves to add huge costs to support huge government bureaucracies. If government controlled healthcare, it would initiate rationing. This is the only way they know to control costs. The result will be less healthcare to go around. The quality of healthcare will decline. An 80 year old mother, who needs a new hip, won't get one because the 'invisible' bureaucrats will not allow Mom's doctor to provide such expensive care. A Dad who gets cancer will be allowed to die rather than stretching out his life with expensive treatments. The current legislative proposals before Congress specifically provide that once someone reaches the age of 65, bureaucrats will mandate counseling designed to advise them on available options regarding their future. This is, in essence, indoctrinating them on the benefits of rationing and euthanasia once they become very sick.

This power will be in the hands of the 'nanny state', rather than with the patient and the family. The Obama administration does not believe in empowering individuals. It believes that everything should be governed out of Washington, DC, and that politicians are better able to make decisions for the patient and their family than they can. This is socialism! Karl Marx would be proud.

Let's look at the facts. Liberals tell us we must have universal healthcare because it is a moral obligation of a great nation like ours, and 47 million people in the U.S. are without healthcare. Wow! Hard to argue that, but is this true? We never hear the media pundits question these facts. Are 47 million Americans uninsured? No. The real number is considerably lower, probably about 18 million Americans. Why do we hear the number 47 million in political campaign after political campaign? Because politicians can never tell us the truth. Truth doesn't matter anymore. What they say is always about spinning facts that will benefit the policies they are pushing on us.

The Obama administration reached its figure of 47 million using creative math. There are 18 million uninsured, however, the government also includes in its yearly analysis all those who are between jobs. In other words, if I am out of a job for one week, thereby losing healthcare coverage for that one week, even though the following week I am re-employed and get new coverage, the government considers me as one of the 47 million uninsured. In addition, many Americans are offered healthcare insurance by their employers but "choose" not to have coverage, thereby maximizing their take home pay. This is America after all. Are we not currently allowed to "choose" whether we want insurance coverage? Most of the Americans who choose not to have coverage tend to be the youngest and healthiest of us. A 25 year old waiter may choose not to have to pay a few hundred dollars per month for healthcare coverage because they see no reason to. They are healthy and never see a doctor. They would rather use the few hundred dollars per month to buy a car, share an apartment with friends rather than living home with Mom and Dad, or just buy some beers on the weekend or go out on a date. If an emergency does arise, for example, they get in a car accident, they go to the emergency room and get the same care as an insured anyway.

In Obama's America, this will not be allowed to happen. Everyone will be forced to have healthcare so that the government can collect revenue to put toward the massive costs needed to deliver this healthcare to every citizen. Oh, did I say "citizen"? The liberal healthcare reform bills will have American taxpayers paying for free healthcare to 12 million illegal immigrants. How wonderful! Some Republicans have tried to get Congress to amend the legislation so that illegal immigrants can have the crisis care (we won't reject anyone from the emergency room) but these crazy Republicans think the illegal immigrants should at least pay for their healthcare rather than causing American taxpayers to redistribute their hard earned dollars in support of healthcare for people who are not even citizens of this country.

Speaking of emergency room care, everyone who goes to an emergency room in this country gets help. No one is turned away. If they are illegal immigrants, they are cared for. If they have no insurance, they are cared for. If they are felons, they are cared for. If they are tourists, they are cared for. If they are young, old, black, white, male, female or anything else, they are cared for. Doesn't this mean we already have universal health coverage?

Another amazing piece of dishonesty around this healthcare reform debate is that it won't cost you anything. How can that be? The plan is to insure 47 million more people and stuff them into the current system. 47 million more people using the same number of doctors and nurses, and the same number of clinics and hospitals. What fantasy world do Liberals live in where 47 million more people can use the same infrastructure and yet have no impact on delivery of the services? There will be an inevitable push and pull. The result will be patients being treated like a number in a vast government system. Patients will experience a longer wait time to see the doctor and a longer time to get

Manifesto of Common Sense

treatment once finally diagnosed. These delays can, and will, have a material adverse effect on the healthcare of many of us.

Consider the Department of Motor Vehicles. A typical wait is 45 minutes to finally get up to a clerk's window. A clerk, who barely looks up, gives you a form, tells you to go to the side of the room and complete the form and then stand in another line and hand in your completed form to another clerk. Like the sheep that you are, you follow the clerk's instructions. Of course, when you go to the side of the room, you have to wait ten minutes to get a spot to fill out your form. You finally find a spot but there is no pen, or the pen has no ink. Eventually, you find some other sheepish person to lend you a pen. The wait in the second line is an additional 30 minutes. You get to the front of the line and the second clerk barely looks up at you, takes your form and tells you that you did not fill it out correctly and you have to go back to the side of the room and complete it properly this time. Of course, there is no staff person at the side of the room to help answer any questions you might have regarding the form, so you are left to scratch your head and hope that you are doing it right this time, or maybe you ask the nice person who lent you a pen for help. You stand in line again, and clerk #2 sighs at how stupid you are because the form is still not filled out right. Now you plead for assistance. clerk #2, after uttering another loud sigh so as to embarrass you, gives you a clue as to how the form is to be completed and allows you to make the final change to the form at the window. Now the form is finally accepted by clerk #2 and you are told to go back to your seat and wait to be called by another clerk. You go to your dirty plastic seat, with gum stuck on the back, and do your best not to touch anything. Fifteen more minutes go by and a third clerk calls you up, takes your photo and the process is finally done.

This may sound funny when you read it, but this is essentially the healthcare system the Liberals are promising you. The cost for this deluxe service will be significantly higher than anything you can currently imagine. The State of Massachusetts is going bankrupt trying to support the healthcare plan they passed just a few years ago. The healthcare plans in Congress have a great deal in common with what the State of Massachusetts has. This "test" market is a great place to see the reality that will come to your front door. The State of Tennessee tried universal healthcare in 1994. Shortly after adopting it, they had to nix it. Tennessee had estimated it would cost $2 billion dollars. It quickly ballooned to $8 billion dollars. Tennessee had significantly underestimated the number of people that would give up their private health plans and jump on the public option plan. Sure, once it was free from the government, why should one pay for their own insurance plan? The large number of people leaving the private health plans forced the insurance companies that offered private health insurance to cut benefits and increase premiums when the pool of people paying for private insurance decreased so dramatically, causing even more people to leave the private insurance plans and take the public option. Private insurance could not compete with the public option.

These arguments should sound familiar to you. It is exactly the same argument you hear every night on the evening news about the federal healthcare plan. Yet the media, which supports Obama and the destruction of America, fail to tell us about the problems in Canada, the UK, France, and even in our own country in states like Massachusetts, Maine, Hawaii and Tennessee. This is not an abstract intellectual argument. The healthcare experiment has been undertaken and has failed miserably in every venue where it was tried. If our politicians or mainstream media were to educate Americans on the real effects the reform bill will have on the population, the reform bills would never get out of committee, let alone pass Congress and become law. Liberals are simply not interested in bringing about real healthcare reform. They are interested in acquiring power which means redistributing your income for plans that provide them with more power. They truly believe they are smarter than you and therefore they should decide on how best to spend your money, whether it is on education, healthcare or decisions affecting your business or other aspects of your daily life.

President Obama is being disingenuous at best when he tells Americans they will be able to keep their private insurance. He knows better. He is being disingenuous when he says it will be deficit neutral. Congressman Rangel wants a surtax on millionaires to help pay for the healthcare reform. There are not enough rich people in America to pay for the healthcare for everyone. The problem in making millionaires pay an additional 5% of their income is that it will not generate enough money to pay for the plan. There are not enough millionaires in the United States which means non-millionaires will be burdened with the bulk of the paying. If one assumes the millionaires are stupid, (knowing they did not become millionaires by being stupid,) it's

Healthcare Reform—What This is Really All About

a simple fact that 1% of our population cannot afford to provide healthcare for the other 99%. One must assume that millionaires are stupid if one assumes millionaires will not find ways to shelter their income, if not just move out of the country altogether, in order to avoid paying exorbitant taxes in the range of 60%-70% of their earnings. Accordingly, we will have a declining population of rich people to kick around. Where they go, their money will follow. Where they go, jobs will be created. Jobs will be lost in America. Good idea, President Obama! Is this the change we can believe in: a declining growth rate in America to support higher growth rates in other countries? Yes, I believe this is what President Obama really wants. He believes America should not be any better than any other country. When our economic wealth declines in preference of other countries, we can all be equally poor. But I digress. The estimated cost of healthcare reform, as currently proposed, is in the neighborhood of $1.3 **Trillion** dollars. Recall the experience in Tennessee where they estimated $2 billion but it quickly ballooned to $8 billion. You can bet we will experience the same thing with healthcare reform. In fact, we have always seen the same ballooning of costs in Medicare and Medicaid. It is just one of those facts in life you can always count on. Everything will always cost more than you estimate.

With the healthcare reform bills as proposed by Liberals, our government will control approximately another 20% of the American economy. Another 20%! Remember, they already regulate just about every other industry. They control education, road building, security, defense, and most aspects of our everyday life. With healthcare control in the hands of our government, the government will have power over the most personal of human decisions: how to take care of ourselves and our family. Will the government decide that obese people cost our healthcare system too much so they need to mandate appropriate weight limits for its citizens? Will it mandate that every citizen must spend a minimum of 4 hours per week in the gym exercising? Will it mandate what type of food our stores and restaurants are allowed to serve and sell? Will it mandate when it is time to pull the proverbial "plug" on my life because the cost of keeping me alive is more than some snot-nosed bureaucrat wants to pay for treatment? The answer to all of these questions are yes, if they want to. This is the concern. The invisible bureaucrat will decide these questions for me. I will no longer have the freedom or liberty as a citizen of the United States to make these simple decisions for myself or my family. George Washington and John Adams are most certainly rolling over in their graves!

I grew up in a generation that allowed me to witness a quality of life among senior citizens that is without comparison in the history of the world. I live in Florida, a state known for having more than its fair share of senior citizens. Every day, I see senior citizens playing golf, tennis, croquet, boating, fishing and endless other activities. I see them enjoying the fruits of having worked hard their whole life and now enjoying their retirement. The primary reason they are able to enjoy these daily activities in their life is a direct result of the success of the greatest healthcare system the world has ever seen. The American healthcare system has not only extended life for the elderly, but more importantly, our healthcare system has delivered a better quality of life. The elderly person whose hip or knee has given out can now have it replaced and, once replaced, they are as good as new and return to an active lifestyle. In turn, the active lifestyle provides a source of positive mental health. They are active with friends and their spouses. They feel better about themselves and good mental health contributes to good physical health and vice versa. This is lost on our Liberal friends. When do you ever see anyone in the media or Congress ever say something positive about a healthcare system that has allowed our parents to actually enjoy their senior years, all with a quality of life that was unimaginable just two or three decades ago?

Read the healthcare bill. Your mother who has arthritis in her knees will have to live with the pain. She will be confined to her home and will have to give up her active life. She will lose the positive influence of friends and a healthy social environment. She will become depressed. Her health will follow a downward spiral. And our new bureaucrats will continue to delay treatments to help her until she dies. But the healthcare system will appear more efficient because it did not spend a lot of money on some old lady. The Liberals will be happy.

Read the healthcare bill. It mandates that taxpayers pay for free abortions, whether you believe in abortions or not. The government won't have money to pay for your Mom to have her arthritic knee replaced but it will have plenty of money to pay for abortions for teenagers, and without the requirement of notifying the teenager's parents that their child is even considering this option.

Read the healthcare bill. It establishes an Office of Minority Health which reports to the Office of Civil Rights. I thought healthcare was supposed to be based on treating the individual who is sick. It is clear our Congress has other ideas, otherwise why would anyone need an Office of Minority Health? The purpose of this new bureaucracy is to provide preferences for minorities. In other words, it is affirmative action for minorities relative to the delivery of healthcare to minorities. In the Liberal healthcare reform bill, healthcare is not about providing equal treatment for one's illness but somehow a bureaucracy whose sole purpose is to ensure minorities get preferential treatment in the delivery of healthcare is a core principle. How come we don't have an Office of White People's Health? Or perhaps an Office for the health of Italian-Americans should be made a part of this healthcare reform movement. After all, it is common knowledge that Italians, like me, drink too much wine so we need to have our own office of bureaucrats to make sure health conditions related to drinking too much wine are studied more than, let's say, cancer research because Italian-Americans have less cancer incidents. In fact, once we have our new office of bureaucrats determine that not enough of your tax dollars are going to study the effects of me drinking too much wine, then I can sue under the guise of the Office of Civil Rights, which will have a central role to play according to the current healthcare bill. I will win a big judgment, and then not to have work anymore and I can stay home, while you work to pay taxes, and I can drink even more wine. Yeah, that is fair! Maybe I should seriously reconsider this socialism stuff.

This is not to suggest that some reform is not necessary. We do need reform. However, reform can be accomplished through the private sector without adding layers of government agencies policing our healthcare. Health insurance should be made more portable. Health insurance should not be terminated due to pre-existing conditions. Individuals need to better understand the costs of health care so that they shop for health care in a manner similar to how they shop for other products or services. Individuals are great shoppers, they seek bargains and force competition. This needs to be carried into healthcare.

Here are some suggestions for reform that actually will reduce costs while not taking away the freedom and liberty individuals currently have to make decisions regarding their own healthcare.

- Subsidize healthcare. If the government wants to incentivize citizens to have healthcare, they can subsidize healthcare by providing individuals with tax credits on their tax returns. This reduces the cost to an individual but retains the decision making to the individual on how to take care of their own health. It may also expand the number of people who buy insurance, thus spreading the cost to more people and reducing costs on an individual basis. This may be a good way to get some of those who choose to be uninsured to decide to get insurance, thereby benefitting the rest of us who already pay for insurance.
- Medical Savings Account. Let Americans save money on a tax-free basis for the purpose of spending it on healthcare. Again, this empowers the individual, not our bureaucrats.
- Mandate transition from paper records to electronic records.

- Tort reform. No serious healthcare reform bill can ignore the enormous costs placed on healthcare arising from the abuse of medical malpractice claims.
- Eliminate fraud currently permeating the entire healthcare industry. Recent studies project $70-$120 billion per year exists just in Medicare and Medicaid fraud. As an example, pizza parlors in Florida claimed they were an HIV clinic, got approved, AND were paid by our government for HIV treatments. The amount of fraud is ridiculously high and any healthcare reform package must provide Americans with assurances that our government will watch over our taxpayer dollars much more diligently than ever before and put an end to the extensive fraud.
- Create regional, or statewide, insurance pools. Insurance pools will allow individuals to participate in large groups to pick up the benefit of reduced costs that come from being part of a large group. This would be very beneficial to individuals and small businesses that get stuck with higher premiums because they are not part of larger pool.
- Make insurance portable so you can take it with you wherever you are employed.

One last thing you need to know about this debate. If Congress passes healthcare, it will not take effect until 2013. Why, if they pass the legislation in 2009, do we have to wait until 2013 to get the benefits of this wonderful program? The answer is because our Liberals understand Americans are not going to

Healthcare Reform—What This is Really All About

like the 'Change' once it is forced upon them. They want to make sure they have the 2010 election and 2012 election behind them, ensuring Democrats maintain political control over our government until 2016. By then it will be too late for Americans to elect a government that can fix this massive boondoggle.

One more last thing. The healthcare being forced upon you is not applicable to our government. They get to keep the tremendous plan we so generously pay for as taxpayers. I guess the plan for us is not that great after all; otherwise our politicians would be making sure they dump their current plan in favor of what they are mandating for us.

The plan being sought by our Liberal Congressman can basically be summed up as follows:

1. Pass Healthcare reform in a manner that let's liberals rule every aspect of every American's life. This is the power grab.
2. Once the power grab occurs, then "re-educate" (I really mean 'brain wash'), Americans on the need to reduce costs because the federal deficit will have ballooned to proportions unimaginable just a few years ago.
3. Reducing costs in healthcare is not difficult. It requires rationing and less use of technology and less research and development of new drugs.
4. By rationing healthcare, the elderly, more than any other segment of the population, will receive less care and thus will die younger. Additionally, the quality of life of our seniors will drop dramatically so the elderly in our society will be ready to die earlier.

5. Now, here comes the ultimate evil of healthcare reform as proposed by our Liberal friends. It solves the Social Security and Medicare problems plaguing our federal deficit. If elderly Americans are "forced," through lack of care, to die earlier, well, less retirement benefits and less Medicare outlays occur.

This is why Liberals are the biggest enemy our country faces and they must be defeated. Their plan to re-invent America will have far reaching changes to the fabric of our daily lives in the most negative way possible. They have shredded the meaning of our Constitution in the process and will continue to do so to achieve their goal of destroying our America. Remember, health care reform is first and foremost about the Democratic Party making the citizens of the U.S. dependent on the largest entitlement program this country has ever seen, which in turn, is very, very positive for the long term prospects of the Democratic Party. Every other argument being made in favor of government run healthcare is a façade for this one over powering goal - the conquest of the Democratic Party regardless of its impact on America. We, the silent majority, need to rise up and have our voices heard at the election polls.

CHAPTER THIRTEEN
WHY OUR POLITICIANS (OF EITHER PARTY) ARE OUR ENEMIES IN THE FIGHT TO RESTORE AMERICA

THE DAY-TO-DAY BLAME GAMES, THE DAILY SPIN GAMES, THE DAILY POLLS, THE POLITICAL CORRECTNESS, THE SELFISHNESS OF PUTTING THEIR RE-ELECTION ABOVE THE COUNTRY'S INTERESTS, THE SEAT OF THEIR PANTS GOVERNING, THE FAILURE TO BE HONEST ABOUT PROBLEMS OR THE REAL CAUSE OF THE PROBLEMS, THE BLOVIATING THAT EVERY PROBLEM IS ALWAYS SOMEONE'S FAULT, THE FEIGNED OUTRAGE THEY LOVE TO EXHIBIT, THE FAILURE TO READ LEGISLATION THEY FORCE ON ALL OF US, THE FAILURE TO DELIBERATE LEGISLATION IN ANY THOUGHTFUL WAY, AND MORE. ALL COLLUDE TO MAKE IT DIFFICULT IF NOT IMPOSSIBLE TO MAKE PROGRESS ON ANY SERIOUS ISSUES.

Why our politicians are our enemies in the fight to restore America

As I have pointed out, I believe most Americans want the same things in life. Most Americans will agree on what we want to see in terms of quality of life, security of our nation, education of our children, health care, secure retirement and other issues. We disagree, for the most part, only on the best way to achieve these things we all want in life for ourselves and for our children. Debate is healthy.

The problem is that our politicians are not leaders. For the most part they are weak-kneed children with only one overriding interest—their desire to get re-elected to feed their over-reaching egos. Both of these things get in the way of doing what is best for the country. Our politicians do not have the strength to do what is right for us. We must remove them from power. We must limit their time of service. People should serve because they want to contribute to America's greatness. Nowadays our politicians are mostly professional politicians. It is all they have ever done. Few have spent any time in the real world. Few have ever worked real jobs, built real businesses or otherwise contributed to our country in a productive way. Many come out of school, get involved in politics and then spend their lives on the public dole with no real sense of how difficult it is for most Americans in the everyday world. Our politicians have become our enemies. John Edwards was right. There are two Americas, just not the two Americas John Edwards saw. The one America is the political class that has high pay, low hours of work, the greatest health care and retirement benefits the world could imagine, celebrity status which treats them like royalty, world class vacations paid by taxpayers, and numerous other fringe benefits. Then there are the rest of us. We work to support the political class so that they can criticize us, tax us, regulate us and do everything in their power to inhibit our ability to progress. If you are rich like the Kennedy family, that is okay, even if your family money came from the illegal activities of your granddad. If you are middle class or upper middle class and you try to improve your position in life and seek to enrich yourself and your family, then you are treated as bad, greedy, and immoral. You must be stopped. The upward mobility in economic classes that built this country is being torn down in the name of our new national religion—redistribution of your earnings. And they are not done, after they take 60% of your income while you are alive, they then will take more from your family when you die. The appetite of Liberals to take your money is insatiable because their need for your money is greater, in their minds, then your need to have your own money.

CHAPTER FOURTEEN
CALL TO ACTION
FIRE THEM!

There is no other solution. Until we take responsibility for the future of our country, you can be sure our politicians won't. It is only through the power of the ballot box that politicians learn to represent the best interests of our country as opposed to their individual interests. It is time to fire them. All of them, if need be. Obama is right, this country needs change. Major change. But not the kind of change he is creating that will produce a stronger political class that will just suck more and more life out of our economy at the expense of the working class that produces the wealth in our country.

How worried are you that socialist countries in Europe and the communist country of China are lecturing America against the Obama economic plan? You should be very worried. These countries have been down this road and have realized that it is a dead end to prosperity. Why don't the liberals in our country understand that everything they desire to do to our economy has been tried and it failed every single place it was ried? Why are the liberals in Congress and Obama so willing to risk the future of America? The world is telling Obama that it cannot afford his plan to spend trillions of dollars. The risk of doing so can bankrupt America and, if that happens, it significantly injures the world economy in the process. World leaders are worried; you should be also.

Obama should visit hospitals in the United Kingdom and Canada to witness how healthcare run by clerks in huge bureaucracies is worse than the health care we currently have. Patient care is rationed in these countries. People die prematurely in these countries due to the rationed care. The overall quality of healthcare is less than what the US has. The cost of healthcare in nations that provide it to their citizens is no less than America – although the citizens of these countries may not realize that since the costs are buried in government spending. I don't know about you, but I am not looking forward to healthcare delivered to us the same way the motor vehicle department delivers services to us. Can you imagine? Our country cannot afford the trillions of tax dollars this will cost and I can't believe Americans will tolerate receiving substandard care.

Every generation of Americans has been able to look forward to their children having a better quality of life than the past generation. Current economic policies are destroying this chance for our children. In the time period from October 2008 thru February 2009, America lost perhaps half its net worth. No one is currently sure how much wealth we really have lost because no one has any idea what our assets are worth, but it is clear that most Americans lost ten years of savings in just a few months. The prognosis is that it will take years and years to recover this lost wealth. The politicians have prescribed tripling the US debt in the next ten years and the problem gets worse from there.

There is no way our children will be able to afford to pay this debt back. It is projected that just the interest on the new debt Congress and Obama have just passed will cost us $850 billion dollars per year. Our dollar will have no value. We will see huge inflationary pressures. Our income and asset value, measured against the pending inflation, will be decreasing. We will be forced to overpay for government programs that provide dismal levels of service. We will have our government intruding into every aspect of our lives. We will have politicians and bureaucrats that will have so much power and authority that they will decide who the winners and losers will be in our economy. Did central planning of government with its five-year plans work in Russia or China? No. It will not work here either. The economies of Russia and China did not start becoming meaningful in the world economy until they discarded five-year planning and freed up capitalist policies inside their countries. Obama is positioning the US to be a Marxist-like economy. His stimulus package is not a short-term stimulus to help us get out of the recession early. Rather, he has intentionally designed it to bring about systemic new government spending at every conceivable level for the next several decades, spending we will not be able to escape from once it has started. Have you ever seen a government program disappear after it has begun?

Call to Action

Yes, I said Marxist. Obama is a Marxist. Pelosi is a Marxist. Let's call this what it is. They are so far left of liberal that they are the biggest danger to America, and to the entire world's economy. Obama made clear during his presidential campaign that he wanted to redistribute American wealth. That is a Marxist ideal. Obama has counseled our children not to get MBAs, or become investment bankers, because he believes the future lies in being community activists and bureaucrats that work for him in his new world order where government has almost totalitarian powers. This is Marxism. Obama wants to decide how much executives get paid. This is Marxism. He wants his treasury to be able to take over (nationalize) any business that the treasury decides is necessary to further the interests of our government. This is Marxism. Obama is taking America to the land of Marxism. Next, Obama will tell us he needs to bail out our failing newspapers, which will mean the government will own the news media and, to a large extent, control their content. Oh, I'm sorry, I forgot that the Liberals already control the news content, so Obama can skip this part of his plan.

They are shredding our Constitution and the laws of our country as they grab power to 'reinvent' America as a socialist society. Hard working people are the enemy. Being upper middle-class or, even worse, rich, is now practically considered a crime in the Obama administration. People who are productive, create wealth, and create jobs are now in the unenviable position of being penalized by our government for their success. Our government cannot allow individualism to prosper because it is the enemy of government's desire to control the masses in all aspects of their lives.

God save us! We need to take unprecedented action. It is time for a new revolution in this country. Take back our government at every level, in our cities, counties, states and, of course, federal levels. Throw out any and all politicians who back the Marxist society Obama and Pelosi have brought to America. Act fast. Our politicians are producing these new laws and regulations with unprecedented speed. Your vote does count. Our Constitution is in danger. Our future is in danger. Our children may for the first time inherit a country on the decline. Our politicians are stupid, selfish and blind to the lessons of history. Obama is right. It is time for a change – a big one. Just a few months of his policies has opened our eyes as to why we have rejected these policies for the last fifty years.

In the past I was not a supporter of term limits. Now I believe we need term limits on all politicians to save our country, at every level of government. We cannot allow our politicians to work in government for their entire life. Professional politicians believe too much in themselves and too little in their constituents. They lose touch with reality of working in a productive job all day, every day. They lose touch with the struggles to survive, get ahead or otherwise seeking to improve your lot in life. They become too powerful and become subject to corrupting influences. They forget where they came from. They believe they are smarter than us, know better than us, and have the right to tell us how to live our lives.

I believe we need term limits to ensure fresh ideas, to ensure the people who lead us are grounded in recent reality and, since they will know they are only in power for a short time, they will be incentivized to do the right thing for the country as opposed to the right thing for themselves so that they can be re-elected. I believe no politician should serve more than two terms in office.

I am as guilty as being apathetic as anyone. Yes, I vote regularly. But I have not written my politicians. I have never called a radio station. I have never written a letter to the editor. I have stood by and watched. I deserve the incompetent lying politicians we have as much as anyone. But I can't stand it anymore. I am disgusted at witnessing the destruction of the great country I inherited from our fathers and forefathers. I need to do better, and so must you. Stand up and make noise.

Let's use capitalism to make us socially compassionate. But let's not make us into a bankrupt Marxist society, no matter how much the fine words of our articulate politicians tell us we need this to survive.

Take charge of our future now. Wake up! It is very nearly too late!

Write your congressman, write your senators, write the leaders of the House and Senate, write your state officials, including your Governor and state representatives, write your county commissioner, mayor and local council members. They must hear from us and, if they don't listen, then organize your friends and neighbors to oppose them and support candidates who agree to take the actions we need to restore this country to the greatness it has always had. This must be done at the grass roots level. If America were a corporation, the shareholders would have fired management a long time ago. This is what we must do. FIRE THEM!

FIRE THE SCHOOL BOARD. FIRE THE COUNTY COMMISSIONERS. FIRE THE MAYOR AND TOWN COUNCILS. FIRE THE STATE LEGISLATORS. FIRE THE U.S. CONGRESSMEN. FIRE THE U.S. SENATORS. FIRE THEM. IT IS YOUR CHOICE. TAKE ACTION AND FIRE THEM ALL OR LOSE AMERICA.

At the Brink of Being Lost

APPENDIX
U.S. CONSTITUTION

- Preamble
- Article 1 - The Legislative Branch
    - Section 1 - The Legislature
    - Section 2 - The House
    - Section 3 - The Senate
    - Section 4 - Elections, Meetings
    - Section 5 - Membership, Rules, Journals, Adjournment
    - Section 6 - Compensation
    - Section 7 - Revenue Bills, Legislative Process, Presidential Veto
    - Section 8 - Powers of Congress
    - Section 9 - Limits on Congress
    - Section 10 - Powers Prohibited of States
- Article 2 - The Executive Branch
    - Section 1 - The President
    - Section 2 - Civilian Power over Military, Cabinet, Pardon Power, Appointments

Appendix: U.S. Constitution

- - Section 3 - State of the Union, Convening Congress
  - Section 4 - Disqualification
- Article 3 - The Judicial Branch
  - Section 1 - Judicial Powers
  - Section 2 - Trial by Jury, Original Jurisdiction, Jury Trials
  - Section 3 - Treason
- Article 4 - The States
  - Section 1 - Each State to Honor All Others
  - Section 2 - State Citizens, Extradition
  - Section 3 - New States
  - Section 4 - Republican Government
- Article 5 - Amendment
- Article 6 - Debts, Supremacy, Oaths
- Article 7 - Ratification
- Signatories
- Amendments
  - Amendment 1 - Freedom of Religion, Press, Expression
  - Amendment 2 - Right to Bear Arms
  - Amendment 3 - Quartering of Soldiers
  - Amendment 4 - Search and Seizure
  - Amendment 5 - Trial and Punishment, Compensation for Takings
  - Amendment 6 - Right to Speedy Trial, Confrontation of Witnesses
  - Amendment 7 - Trial by Jury in Civil Cases

- Amendment 8 - Cruel and Unusual Punishment
- Amendment 9 - Construction of Constitution
- Amendment 10 - Powers of the States and People
- Amendment 11 - Judicial Limits
- Amendment 12 - Choosing the President, Vice President
- Amendment 13 - Slavery Abolished
- Amendment 14 - Citizenship Rights
- Amendment 15 - Race No Bar to Vote
- Amendment 16 - Status of Income Tax Clarified
- Amendment 17 - Senators Elected by Popular Vote
- Amendment 18 - Liquor Abolished
- Amendment 19 - Women's Suffrage
- Amendment 20 - Presidential, Congressional Terms
- Amendment 21 - Amendment 18 Repealed
- Amendment 22 - Presidential Term Limits
- Amendment 23 - Presidential Vote for District of Columbia
- Amendment 24 - Poll Taxes Barred
- Amendment 25 - Presidential Disability and Succession
- Amendment 26 - Voting Age Set to 18 Years
- Amendment 27 - Limiting Congressional Pay Increases

Appendix: U.S. Constitution

The Constitution of the United States

Preamble

We the People of the United States, in Order to form a more perfect Union, establish Justice, insure domestic Tranquility, provide for the common defence, promote the general Welfare, and secure the Blessings of Liberty to ourselves and our Posterity, do ordain and establish this Constitution for the United States of America.

Article I - The Legislative Branch

Section 1 - The Legislature

All legislative Powers herein granted shall be vested in a Congress of the United States, which shall consist of a Senate and House of Representatives.

Section 2 - The House

The House of Representatives shall be composed of Members chosen every second Year by the People of the several States, and the Electors in each State shall have the Qualifications requisite for Electors of the most numerous Branch of the State Legislature.

No Person shall be a Representative who shall not have attained to the Age of twenty five Years, and been seven Years a Citizen of the United States, and who shall not, when elected, be an Inhabitant of that State in which he shall be chosen.

(Representatives and direct Taxes shall be <u>apportioned</u> among the several States which may be included within this Union, according to their respective Numbers, which shall be determined by adding to the whole Number of free Persons, including those bound to Service for a Term of Years, and excluding Indians not taxed, three fifths of all other Persons.) **(The previous sentence in parentheses was modified by the <u>14th Amendment, section 2</u>.)** The actual <u>Enumeration</u> shall be made within three Years after the first Meeting of the Congress of the United States, and within every subsequent Term of ten Years, in such Manner as they shall by Law direct. The Number of Representatives shall not exceed one for every thirty Thousand, but each State shall have at Least one Representative; and until such <u>enumeration</u> shall be made, the State of New Hampshire shall be entitled to <u>chuse</u> three, Massachusetts eight, Rhode Island and Providence Plantations one, Connecticut five, New York six, New Jersey four, Pennsylvania eight, Delaware one, Maryland six, Virginia ten, North Carolina five, South Carolina five and Georgia three.

When vacancies happen in the Representation from any State, the Executive Authority thereof shall issue Writs of Election to fill such Vacancies.

The House of Representatives shall choose their Speaker and other Officers; and shall have the sole Power of Impeachment.

Section 3 - The Senate

The Senate of the United States shall be composed of two Senators from each State, *(chosen by the Legislature thereof,)* **(The preceding**

Appendix: U.S. Constitution

words in parentheses superseded by 17th Amendment, section 1.) for six Years; and each Senator shall have one Vote.

Immediately after they shall be assembled in Consequence of the first Election, they shall be divided as equally as may be into three Classes. The Seats of the Senators of the first Class shall be vacated at the Expiration of the second Year, of the second Class at the Expiration of the fourth Year, and of the third Class at the Expiration of the sixth Year, so that one third may be chosen every second Year; *(and if Vacancies happen by Resignation, or otherwise, during the Recess of the Legislature of any State, the Executive thereof may make temporary Appointments until the next Meeting of the Legislature, which shall then fill such Vacancies.)* **(The preceding words in parentheses were superseded by the 17th Amendment, section 2.)**

No person shall be a Senator who shall not have attained to the Age of thirty Years, and been nine Years a Citizen of the United States, and who shall not, when elected, be an Inhabitant of that State for which he shall be chosen.

The Vice President of the United States shall be President of the Senate, but shall have no Vote, unless they be equally divided.

The Senate shall choose their other Officers, and also a President pro tempore, in the absence of the Vice President, or when he shall exercise the Office of President of the United States.

The Senate shall have the sole Power to try all Impeachments. When sitting for that Purpose, they shall be on Oath or Affirmation. When the President of the United States is tried, the Chief Justice shall preside: And no Person shall be convicted without the Concurrence of two thirds of the Members present.

Judgment in Cases of Impeachment shall not extend further than to removal from Office, and disqualification to hold and enjoy any Office of honor, Trust or Profit under the United States: but the Party convicted shall nevertheless be liable and subject to Indictment, Trial, Judgment and Punishment, according to Law.

Section 4 - Elections, Meetings

The Times, Places and Manner of holding Elections for Senators and Representatives, shall be prescribed in each State by the Legislature thereof; but the Congress may at any time by Law make or alter such Regulations, except as to the Place of Chusing Senators.

The Congress shall assemble at least once in every Year, and such Meeting shall *(be on the first Monday in December,)* **(The preceding words in parentheses were superseded by the 20th Amendment, section 2.**) unless they shall by Law appoint a different Day.

Section 5 - Membership, Rules, Journals, Adjournment

Each House shall be the Judge of the Elections, Returns and Qualifications of its own Members, and a Majority of each shall constitute a Quorum to do Business; but a smaller number may adjourn from day to day, and may be authorized to compel the Attendance of absent Members, in such Manner, and under such Penalties as each House may provide.

Each House may determine the Rules of its Proceedings, punish its Members for disorderly Behavior, and, with the Concurrence of two-thirds, expel a Member.

Each House shall keep a Journal of its Proceedings, and from time to time publish the same, excepting such Parts as may in their Judgment require Secrecy; and the Yeas and Nays of the Members of either House on any question shall, at the Desire of one fifth of those Present, be entered on the Journal.

Neither House, during the Session of Congress, shall, without the Consent of the other, <u>adjourn</u> for more than three days, nor to any other Place than that in which the two Houses shall be sitting.

Section 6 - Compensation

(The Senators and Representatives shall receive a Compensation for their Services, to be ascertained by Law, and paid out of the Treasury of the United States.) **(The preceding words in parentheses were modified by the <u>27th Amendment</u>.)** They shall in all Cases, except Treason, Felony and Breach of the Peace, be privileged from Arrest during their Attendance at the Session of their respective Houses, and in going to and returning from the same; and for any Speech or Debate in either House, they shall not be questioned in any other Place.

No Senator or Representative shall, during the Time for which he was elected, be appointed to any civil Office under the Authority of the United States which shall have been created, or the Emoluments whereof shall have been increased during such time; and no Person holding any Office under the United States, shall be a Member of either House during his Continuance in Office.

Section 7 - Revenue Bills, Legislative Process, Presidential Veto

All bills for raising Revenue shall originate in the House of Representatives; but the Senate may propose or concur with Amendments as on other Bills.

Every Bill which shall have passed the House of Representatives and the Senate, shall, before it become a Law, be presented to the President of the United States; If he approve he shall sign it, but if not he shall return it, with his Objections to that House in which it shall have originated, who shall enter the Objections at large on their Journal, and proceed to reconsider it. If after such Reconsideration two thirds of that House shall agree to pass the Bill, it shall be sent, together with the Objections, to the other House, by which it shall likewise be reconsidered, and if approved by two thirds of that House, it shall become a Law. But in all such Cases the Votes of both Houses shall be determined by Yeas and Nays, and the Names of the Persons voting for and against the Bill shall be entered on the Journal of each House respectively. If any Bill shall not be returned by the President within ten Days (Sundays excepted) after it shall have been presented to him, the Same shall be a Law, in like Manner as if he had signed it, unless the Congress by their Adjournment prevent its Return, in which Case it shall not be a Law.

Every Order, Resolution, or Vote to which the Concurrence of the Senate and House of Representatives may be necessary (except on a question of Adjournment) shall be presented to the President of the United States; and before the Same shall take Effect, shall be approved by him, or being disapproved by him, shall be repassed by two thirds of the Senate and House of Representatives, according to the Rules and Limitations prescribed in the Case of a Bill.

Section 8 - Powers of Congress

The Congress shall have Power To lay and collect Taxes, Duties, Imposts and Excises, to pay the Debts and provide for the common Defence and general Welfare of the United States; but all Duties, Imposts and Excises shall be uniform throughout the United States;

To borrow money on the credit of the United States;

To regulate Commerce with foreign Nations, and among the several States, and with the Indian Tribes;

To establish an uniform Rule of Naturalization, and uniform Laws on the subject of Bankruptcies throughout the United States;

To coin Money, regulate the Value thereof, and of foreign Coin, and fix the Standard of Weights and Measures;

To provide for the Punishment of counterfeiting the Securities and current Coin of the United States;

To establish Post Offices and Post Roads;

To promote the Progress of Science and useful Arts, by securing for limited Times to Authors and Inventors the exclusive Right to their respective Writings and Discoveries;

To constitute Tribunals inferior to the supreme Court;

To define and punish Piracies and Felonies committed on the high Seas, and Offenses against the Law of Nations;

To declare War, grant Letters of Marque and Reprisal, and make Rules concerning Captures on Land and Water;

To raise and support Armies, but no Appropriation of Money to that Use shall be for a longer Term than two Years;

To provide and maintain a Navy;

To make Rules for the Government and Regulation of the land and naval Forces;

To provide for calling forth the Militia to execute the Laws of the Union, suppress Insurrections and repel Invasions;

To provide for organizing, arming, and disciplining the Militia, and for governing such Part of them as may be employed in the Service of the United States, reserving to the States respectively, the Appointment of the Officers, and the Authority of training the Militia according to the discipline prescribed by Congress;

To exercise exclusive Legislation in all Cases whatsoever, over such District (not exceeding ten Miles square) as may, by Cession of particular States, and the acceptance of Congress, become the Seat of the Government of the United States, and to exercise like Authority over all Places purchased by the Consent of the Legislature of the State in which the Same shall be, for the Erection of Forts, Magazines, Arsenals, dock-Yards, and other needful Buildings; And

To make all Laws which shall be necessary and proper for carrying into Execution the foregoing Powers, and all other Powers vested by this Constitution in the Government of the United States, or in any Department or Officer thereof.

Section 9 - Limits on Congress

The Migration or Importation of such Persons as any of the States now existing shall think proper to admit, shall not be prohibited by the Congress prior to the Year one thousand eight hundred and eight, but a tax or duty may be imposed on such Importation, not exceeding ten dollars for each Person.

The privilege of the Writ of Habeas Corpus shall not be suspended, unless when in Cases of Rebellion or Invasion the public Safety may require it.

No Bill of Attainder or ex post facto Law shall be passed.

(No capitation, or other direct, Tax shall be laid, unless in Proportion to the Census or <u>Enumeration</u> herein before directed to be taken.) **(Section in parentheses clarified by the <u>16th Amendment</u>.)**

No Tax or Duty shall be laid on Articles exported from any State.

No Preference shall be given by any Regulation of Commerce or Revenue to the Ports of one State over those of another: nor shall

Vessels bound to, or from, one State, be obliged to enter, clear, or pay Duties in another.

No Money shall be drawn from the Treasury, but in Consequence of Appropriations made by Law; and a regular Statement and Account of the Receipts and Expenditures of all public Money shall be published from time to time.

No Title of Nobility shall be granted by the United States: And no Person holding any Office of Profit or Trust under them, shall, without the Consent of the Congress, accept of any present, Emolument, Office, or Title, of any kind whatever, from any King, Prince or foreign State.

Section 10 - Powers prohibited of States

No State shall enter into any Treaty, Alliance, or Confederation; grant Letters of Marque and Reprisal; coin Money; emit Bills of Credit; make any Thing but gold and silver Coin a Tender in Payment of Debts; pass any Bill of Attainder, ex post facto Law, or Law impairing the Obligation of Contracts, or grant any Title of Nobility.

No State shall, without the Consent of the Congress, lay any Imposts or Duties on Imports or Exports, except what may be absolutely necessary for executing it's inspection Laws: and the net Produce of all Duties and Imposts, laid by any State on Imports or Exports, shall be for the Use of the Treasury of the United States; and all such Laws shall be subject to the Revision and Controul of the Congress.

No State shall, without the Consent of Congress, lay any duty of Tonnage, keep Troops, or Ships of War in time of Peace, enter into any Agreement or Compact with another State, or with a foreign Power, or engage in War, unless actually invaded, or in such imminent Danger as will not admit of delay.

Article II - The Executive Branch

Section 1 - The President

The executive Power shall be vested in a President of the United States of America. He shall hold his Office during the Term of four Years, and, together with the Vice-President chosen for the same Term, be elected, as follows:

Each State shall appoint, in such Manner as the Legislature thereof may direct, a Number of Electors, equal to the whole Number of Senators and Representatives to which the State may be entitled in the Congress: but no Senator or Representative, or Person holding an Office of Trust or Profit under the United States, shall be appointed an Elector.

(The Electors shall meet in their respective States, and vote by Ballot for two persons, of whom one at least shall not lie an Inhabitant of the same State with themselves. And they shall make a List of all the Persons voted for, and of the Number of Votes for each; which List they shall sign and certify, and transmit sealed to the Seat of the Government of the United States, directed to the President of the Senate. The President of the Senate shall, in the Presence of the Senate and House of Representatives, open all the Certificates, and the Votes

shall then be counted. The Person having the greatest Number of Votes shall be the President, if such Number be a Majority of the whole Number of Electors appointed; and if there be more than one who have such Majority, and have an equal Number of Votes, then the House of Representatives shall immediately chuse by Ballot one of them for President; and if no Person have a Majority, then from the five highest on the List the said House shall in like Manner chuse the President. But in chusing the President, the Votes shall be taken by States, the Representation from each State having one Vote; a quorum for this Purpose shall consist of a Member or Members from two-thirds of the States, and a Majority of all the States shall be necessary to a Choice. In every Case, after the Choice of the President, the Person having the greatest Number of Votes of the Electors shall be the Vice President. But if there should remain two or more who have equal Votes, the Senate shall chuse from them by Ballot the Vice-President.) **(This clause in parentheses was superseded by the <u>12th Amendment</u>.)**

The Congress may determine the Time of choosing the Electors, and the Day on which they shall give their Votes; which Day shall be the same throughout the United States.

No person except a natural born Citizen, or a Citizen of the United States, at the time of the Adoption of this Constitution, shall be eligible to the Office of President; neither shall any Person be eligible to that Office who shall not have attained to the Age of thirty-five Years, and been fourteen Years a Resident within the United States.

(In Case of the Removal of the President from Office, or of his Death, Resignation, or Inability to discharge the Powers and Duties of

the said Office, the same shall devolve on the Vice President, and the Congress may by Law provide for the Case of Removal, Death, Resignation or Inability, both of the President and Vice President, declaring what Officer shall then act as President, and such Officer shall act accordingly, until the Disability be removed, or a President shall be elected.) **(This clause in parentheses has been modified by the 20th and 25th Amendments.)**

The President shall, at stated Times, receive for his Services, a Compensation, which shall neither be increased nor diminished during the Period for which he shall have been elected, and he shall not receive within that Period any other Emolument from the United States, or any of them.

Before he enter on the Execution of his Office, he shall take the following Oath or Affirmation:

"I do solemnly swear (or affirm) that I will faithfully execute the Office of President of the United States, and will to the best of my Ability, preserve, protect and defend the Constitution of the United States."

Section 2 - Civilian Power over Military, Cabinet, Pardon Power, Appointments

The President shall be Commander in Chief of the Army and Navy of the United States, and of the Militia of the several States, when called into the actual Service of the United States; he may require the Opinion, in writing, of the principal Officer in each of the executive Departments, upon any subject relating to the

Duties of their respective Offices, and he shall have Power to Grant Reprieves and Pardons for Offenses against the United States, except in Cases of Impeachment.

He shall have Power, by and with the Advice and Consent of the Senate, to make Treaties, provided two thirds of the Senators present concur; and he shall nominate, and by and with the Advice and Consent of the Senate, shall appoint Ambassadors, other public Ministers and Consuls, Judges of the supreme Court, and all other Officers of the United States, whose Appointments are not herein otherwise provided for, and which shall be established by Law: but the Congress may by Law vest the Appointment of such inferior Officers, as they think proper, in the President alone, in the Courts of Law, or in the Heads of Departments.

The President shall have Power to fill up all Vacancies that may happen during the Recess of the Senate, by granting Commissions which shall expire at the End of their next Session.

Section 3 - State of the Union, Convening Congress

He shall from time to time give to the Congress Information of the State of the Union, and recommend to their Consideration such Measures as he shall judge necessary and expedient; he may, on extraordinary Occasions, convene both Houses, or either of them, and in Case of Disagreement between them, with Respect to the Time of Adjournment, he may adjourn them to such Time as he shall think proper; he shall receive Ambassadors and other public Ministers; he shall take Care that the Laws be faithfully executed, and shall Commission all the Officers of the United States.

Section 4 - Disqualification

The President, Vice President and all civil Officers of the United States, shall be removed from Office on Impeachment for, and Conviction of, Treason, Bribery, or other high Crimes and Misdemeanors.

Article III - The Judicial Branch

Section 1 - Judicial powers

The judicial Power of the United States, shall be vested in one supreme Court, and in such inferior Courts as the Congress may from time to time ordain and establish. The Judges, both of the supreme and inferior Courts, shall hold their Offices during good Behavior, and shall, at stated Times, receive for their Services a Compensation which shall not be diminished during their Continuance in Office.

Section 2 - Trial by Jury, Original Jurisdiction, Jury Trials

(The judicial Power shall extend to all Cases, in Law and Equity, arising under this Constitution, the Laws of the United States, and Treaties made, or which shall be made, under their Authority; to all Cases affecting Ambassadors, other public Ministers and Consuls; to all Cases of admiralty and maritime Jurisdiction; to Controversies to which the United States shall be a Party; to Controversies between two or more States; between a State and Citizens of another State; between Citizens of different States; between Citizens of the same State claiming Lands under Grants of different States, and between a State,

or the Citizens thereof, and foreign States, Citizens or Subjects.) **(This section in parentheses is modified by the 11th Amendment.)**

In all Cases affecting Ambassadors, other public Ministers and Consuls, and those in which a State shall be Party, the supreme Court shall have original Jurisdiction. In all the other Cases before mentioned, the supreme Court shall have appellate Jurisdiction, both as to Law and Fact, with such Exceptions, and under such Regulations as the Congress shall make.

The Trial of all Crimes, except in Cases of Impeachment, shall be by Jury; and such Trial shall be held in the State where the said Crimes shall have been committed; but when not committed within any State, the Trial shall be at such Place or Places as the Congress may by Law have directed.

Section 3 - Treason

Treason against the United States, shall consist only in levying War against them, or in adhering to their Enemies, giving them Aid and Comfort. No Person shall be convicted of Treason unless on the Testimony of two Witnesses to the same overt Act, or on Confession in open Court.

The Congress shall have power to declare the Punishment of Treason, but no Attainder of Treason shall work Corruption of Blood, or Forfeiture except during the Life of the Person attainted.

Appendix: U.S. Constitution

Article IV - The States

Section 1 - Each State to Honor all others

Full Faith and Credit shall be given in each State to the public Acts, Records, and judicial Proceedings of every other State. And the Congress may by general Laws prescribe the Manner in which such Acts, Records and Proceedings shall be proved, and the Effect thereof.

Section 2 - State citizens, Extradition

The Citizens of each State shall be entitled to all Privileges and Immunities of Citizens in the several States.

A Person charged in any State with Treason, Felony, or other Crime, who shall flee from Justice, and be found in another State, shall on demand of the executive Authority of the State from which he fled, be delivered up, to be removed to the State having Jurisdiction of the Crime.

(No Person held to Service or Labour in one State, under the Laws thereof, escaping into another, shall, in Consequence of any Law or Regulation therein, be discharged from such Service or Labour, But shall be delivered up on Claim of the Party to whom such Service or Labour may be due.) **(This clause in parentheses is superseded by the 13th Amendment.)**

Section 3 - New States

New States may be admitted by the Congress into this Union; but no new States shall be formed or erected within the Jurisdiction of any other State; nor any State be formed by the Junction of two or more States, or parts of States, without the Consent of the Legislatures of the States concerned as well as of the Congress.

The Congress shall have Power to dispose of and make all needful Rules and Regulations respecting the Territory or other Property belonging to the United States; and nothing in this Constitution shall be so construed as to Prejudice any Claims of the United States, or of any particular State.

Section 4 - Republican government

The United States shall guarantee to every State in this Union a Republican Form of Government, and shall protect each of them against Invasion; and on Application of the Legislature, or of the Executive (when the Legislature cannot be convened) against domestic Violence.

Article V - Amendment

The Congress, whenever two thirds of both Houses shall deem it necessary, shall propose Amendments to this Constitution, or, on the Application of the Legislatures of two thirds of the several States, shall call a Convention for proposing Amendments, which, in either Case, shall be valid to all Intents and Purposes, as part of this Constitution, when ratified by the Legislatures of three fourths of the several States, or by Conventions in three fourths thereof, as the one or the other Mode of Ratification may be proposed by the Congress; Provided that no Amendment which may be made prior to the Year One thousand eight hundred and eight shall in any Manner affect the first and fourth Clauses in the Ninth Section of the first Article; and that no State, without its Consent, shall be deprived of its equal Suffrage in the Senate.

Article VI - Debts, Supremacy, Oaths

All Debts contracted and Engagements entered into, before the Adoption of this Constitution, shall be as valid against the United States under this Constitution, as under the Confederation.

This Constitution, and the Laws of the United States which shall be made in Pursuance thereof; and all Treaties made, or which shall be made, under the Authority of the United States, shall be the supreme Law of the Land; and the Judges in every State shall be bound thereby, any Thing in the Constitution or Laws of any State to the Contrary notwithstanding.

The Senators and Representatives before mentioned, and the Members of the several State Legislatures, and all executive and judicial Officers, both of the United States and of the several States, shall be bound by Oath or Affirmation, to support this Constitution; but no religious Test shall ever be required as a Qualification to any Office or public Trust under the United States.

Article VII - Ratification

The Ratification of the Conventions of nine States, shall be sufficient for the Establishment of this Constitution between the States so ratifying the Same.

Done in Convention by the Unanimous Consent of the States present the Seventeenth Day of September in the Year of our Lord one thousand seven hundred and Eighty seven and of the Independence of the United States of America the Twelfth. In Witness whereof We have hereunto subscribed our Names.

George Washington - President and deputy from Virginia

New Hampshire - John Langdon, Nicholas Gilman

Massachusetts - Nathaniel Gorham, Rufus King

Connecticut - Wm Saml Johnson, Roger Sherman

New York - Alexander Hamilton

New Jersey - Wil Livingston, David Brearley, Wm Paterson, Jona. Dayton

Pennsylvania - B Franklin, Thomas Mifflin, Robt Morris, Geo. Clymer, Thos FitzSimons, Jared Ingersoll, James Wilson, Gouv Morris

Delaware - Geo. Read, Gunning Bedford jun, John Dickinson, Richard Bassett, Jaco. Broom

Appendix: U.S. Constitution

Maryland - James McHenry, Dan of St Tho Jenifer, Danl Carroll

Virginia - John Blair, James Madison Jr.

North Carolina - Wm Blount, Richd Dobbs Spaight, Hu Williamson

South Carolina - J. Rutledge, Charles Cotesworth Pinckney, Charles Pinckney, Pierce Butler

Georgia - William Few, Abr Baldwin

Attest: William Jackson, Secretary

The Amendments

The following are the Amendments to the Constitution. The first ten Amendments collectively are commonly known as the <u>Bill of Rights.</u>

Amendment 1 - Freedom of Religion, Press, <u>Expression</u>. <u>Ratified</u> 12/15/1791.

Congress shall make no law respecting an establishment of religion, or prohibiting the free exercise thereof; or abridging the freedom of speech, or of the press; or the right of the people peaceably to assemble, and to petition the Government for a redress of grievances.

Amendment 2 - Right to Bear Arms. <u>Ratified</u> 12/15/1791.

A well regulated Militia, being necessary to the security of a free State, the right of the people to keep and bear Arms, shall not be <u>infringed.</u>

Amendment 3 - Quartering of Soldiers. <u>Ratified</u> 12/15/1791.

No Soldier shall, in time of peace be quartered in any house, without the consent of the Owner, nor in time of war, but in a manner to be prescribed by law.

Amendment 4 - Search and Seizure. <u>Ratified</u> 12/15/1791.

The right of the people to be secure in their persons, houses, papers, and effects, against unreasonable searches and seizures, shall not be violated, and no Warrants shall issue, but upon probable cause, supported by Oath or affirmation, and particularly describing the place to be searched, and the persons or things to be seized.

Amendment 5 - Trial and Punishment, Compensation for Takings. Ratified 12/15/1791.

No person shall be held to answer for a capital, or otherwise infamous crime, unless on a presentment or indictment of a Grand Jury, except in cases arising in the land or naval forces, or in the Militia, when in actual service in time of War or public danger; nor shall any person be subject for the same offense to be twice put in jeopardy of life or limb; nor shall be compelled in any criminal case to be a witness against himself, nor be deprived of life, liberty, or property, without due process of law; nor shall private property be taken for public use, without just compensation.

Amendment 6 - Right to Speedy Trial, Confrontation of Witnesses. Ratified 12/15/1791.

In all criminal prosecutions, the accused shall enjoy the right to a speedy and public trial, by an impartial jury of the State and district wherein the crime shall have been committed, which district shall have been previously ascertained by law, and to be informed of the nature and cause of the accusation; to be confronted with the witnesses against him; to have compulsory process for obtaining witnesses in his favor, and to have the Assistance of Counsel for his defence.

Amendment 7 - Trial by Jury in Civil Cases. <u>Ratified</u> 12/15/1791.

In Suits at common law, where the value in controversy shall exceed twenty dollars, the right of trial by jury shall be preserved, and no fact tried by a jury, shall be otherwise re-examined in any Court of the United States, than according to the rules of the common law.

Amendment 8 - Cruel and Unusual Punishment. <u>Ratified</u> 12/15/1791.

Excessive bail shall not be required, nor excessive fines imposed, nor cruel and unusual punishments inflicted.

Amendment 9 - Construction of Constitution. <u>Ratified</u> 12/15/1791.

The enumeration in the Constitution, of certain rights, shall not be construed to deny or disparage others retained by the people.

Amendment 10 - Powers of the States and People. <u>Ratified</u> 12/15/1791. <u>Note</u>

The powers not delegated to the United States by the Constitution, nor prohibited by it to the States, are reserved to the States respectively, or to the people.

Amendment 11 - Judicial Limits. <u>Ratified</u> 2/7/1795. <u>Note</u> <u>History</u>

The Judicial power of the United States shall not be construed to extend to any suit in law or equity, commenced or prosecuted against one of the United States by Citizens of another State, or by Citizens or Subjects of any Foreign State.

Amendment 12 - Choosing the President, Vice-President. Ratified 6/15/1804.

The Electors shall meet in their respective states, and vote by ballot for President and Vice-President, one of whom, at least, shall not be an inhabitant of the same state with themselves; they shall name in their ballots the person voted for as President, and in distinct ballots the person voted for as Vice-President, and they shall make distinct lists of all persons voted for as President, and of all persons voted for as Vice-President and of the number of votes for each, which lists they shall sign and certify, and transmit sealed to the seat of the government of the United States, directed to the President of the Senate;

The President of the Senate shall, in the presence of the Senate and House of Representatives, open all the certificates and the votes shall then be counted;

The person having the greatest Number of votes for President, shall be the President, if such number be a majority of the whole number of Electors appointed; and if no person have such majority, then from the persons having the highest numbers not exceeding three on the list of those voted for as President, the House of Representatives shall choose immediately, by ballot, the President. But in choosing the President, the votes shall be taken by states, the representation from each state having one vote; a quorum for this purpose shall consist of a member or members from two-thirds of the states, and a majority of all the states shall be necessary to a choice. And if the House of Representatives shall not choose a President whenever the right of choice shall devolve upon them, before the fourth day of March next following, then the Vice-President shall act as President, as in the case of the death or other constitutional disability of the President.

The person having the greatest number of votes as Vice-President, shall be the Vice-President, if such number be a majority of the whole number of Electors appointed, and if no person have a majority, then from the two highest numbers on the list, the Senate shall choose the Vice-President; a quorum for the purpose shall consist of two-thirds of the whole number of Senators, and a majority of the whole number shall be necessary to a choice. But no person constitutionally ineligible to the office of President shall be eligible to that of Vice-President of the United States.

Amendment 13 - Slavery Abolished. <u>Ratified</u> 12/6/1865.

1. Neither slavery nor involuntary servitude, except as a punishment for crime whereof the party shall have been duly convicted, shall exist within the United States, or any place subject to their jurisdiction.
2. Congress shall have power to enforce this article by appropriate legislation.

Amendment 14 - Citizenship Rights. <u>Ratified</u> 7/9/1868.

1. All persons born or naturalized in the United States, and subject to the jurisdiction thereof, are citizens of the United States and of the State wherein they reside. No State shall

make or enforce any law which shall abridge the privileges or immunities of citizens of the United States; nor shall any State deprive any person of life, liberty, or property, without due process of law; nor deny to any person within its jurisdiction the equal protection of the laws.

2. Representatives shall be apportioned among the several States according to their respective numbers, counting the whole number of persons in each State, excluding Indians not taxed. But when the right to vote at any election for the choice of electors for President and Vice-President of the United States, Representatives in Congress, the Executive and Judicial officers of a State, or the members of the Legislature thereof, is denied to any of the male inhabitants of such State, being twenty-one years of age, and citizens of the United States, or in any way abridged, except for participation in rebellion, or other crime, the basis of representation therein shall be reduced in the proportion which the number of such male citizens shall bear to the whole number of male citizens twenty-one years of age in such State.

3. No person shall be a Senator or Representative in Congress, or elector of President and Vice-President, or hold any office, civil or military, under the United States, or under any State, who, having previously taken an oath, as a member of Congress, or as an officer of the United States, or as a member of any State legislature, or as an executive or judicial officer of any State, to support the Constitution of the United States, shall have engaged in insurrection or

rebellion against the same, or given aid or comfort to the enemies thereof. But Congress may by a vote of two-thirds of each House, remove such disability.
4. The validity of the public debt of the United States, authorized by law, including debts incurred for payment of pensions and bounties for services in suppressing insurrection or rebellion, shall not be questioned. But neither the United States nor any State shall assume or pay any debt or obligation incurred in aid of insurrection or rebellion against the United States, or any claim for the loss or emancipation of any slave; but all such debts, obligations and claims shall be held illegal and void.
5. The Congress shall have power to enforce, by appropriate legislation, the provisions of this article.

Amendment 15 - Race No Bar to Vote. <u>Ratified</u> 2/3/1870.

1. The right of citizens of the United States to vote shall not be denied or abridged by the United States or by any State on account of race, color, or previous condition of servitude.
2. The Congress shall have power to enforce this article by appropriate legislation.

Amendment 16 - Status of Income Tax Clarified. <u>Ratified</u> 2/3/1913.

The Congress shall have power to lay and collect taxes on incomes, from whatever source derived, without apportionment among the several States, and without regard to any census or enumeration.

Appendix: Bill of Rights and Amendments to U.S. Constitution

Amendment 17 - Senators Elected by Popular Vote. <u>Ratified</u> 4/8/1913.

The Senate of the United States shall be composed of two Senators from each State, elected by the people thereof, for six years; and each Senator shall have one vote. The electors in each State shall have the qualifications requisite for electors of the most numerous branch of the State legislatures.

When vacancies happen in the representation of any State in the Senate, the executive authority of such State shall issue writs of election to fill such vacancies: Provided, That the legislature of any State may empower the executive thereof to make temporary appointments until the people fill the vacancies by election as the legislature may direct.

This amendment shall not be so construed as to affect the election or term of any Senator chosen before it becomes valid as part of the Constitution.

Amendment 18 - Liquor Abolished. <u>Ratified</u> 1/16/1919. Repealed by <u>Amendment 21</u>, 12/5/1933.
http://www.usconstitution.net/constamnotes.html - Am18

1. After one year from the ratification of this article the manufacture, sale, or transportation of intoxicating liquors within, the importation thereof into, or the exportation thereof from the United States and all territory subject to the jurisdiction thereof for beverage purposes is hereby prohibited.

2. The Congress and the several States shall have concurrent power to enforce this article by appropriate legislation.
3. This article shall be inoperative unless it shall have been ratified as an amendment to the Constitution by the legislatures of the several States, as provided in the Constitution, within seven years from the date of the submission hereof to the States by the Congress.

Amendment 19 - Women's <u>Suffrage</u>. <u>Ratified</u> 8/18/1920.

The right of citizens of the United States to vote shall not be denied or abridged by the United States or by any State on account of sex.

Congress shall have power to enforce this article by appropriate legislation.

Amendment 20 - Presidential, Congressional Terms. <u>Ratified</u> 1/23/1933.

1. The terms of the President and Vice President shall end at noon on the 20th day of January, and the terms of Senators and Representatives at noon on the 3d day of January, of the years in which such terms would have ended if this article had not been ratified; and the terms of their successors shall then begin.
2. The Congress shall assemble at least once in every year, and such meeting shall begin at noon on the 3d day of January, unless they shall by law appoint a different day.
3. If, at the time fixed for the beginning of the term of the President, the President elect shall have died, the Vice

President elect shall become President. If a President shall not have been chosen before the time fixed for the beginning of his term, or if the President elect shall have failed to qualify, then the Vice President elect shall act as President until a President shall have qualified; and the Congress may by law provide for the case wherein neither a President elect nor a Vice President elect shall have qualified, declaring who shall then act as President, or the manner in which one who is to act shall be selected, and such person shall act accordingly until a President or Vice President shall have qualified.

4. The Congress may by law provide for the case of the death of any of the persons from whom the House of Representatives may choose a President whenever the right of choice shall have devolved upon them, and for the case of the death of any of the persons from whom the Senate may choose a Vice President whenever the right of choice shall have devolved upon them.

5. Sections 1 and 2 shall take effect on the 15th day of October following the ratification of this article.

6. This article shall be inoperative unless it shall have been ratified as an amendment to the Constitution by the legislatures of three-fourths of the several States within seven years from the date of its submission.

Amendment 21 - <u>Amendment 18</u> Repealed. <u>Ratified</u> 12/5/1933.

1. The eighteenth article of amendment to the Constitution of the United States is hereby repealed.
2. The transportation or importation into any State, Territory, or possession of the United States for delivery or use therein of intoxicating liquors, in violation of the laws thereof, is hereby prohibited.
3. The article shall be inoperative unless it shall have been ratified as an amendment to the Constitution by conventions in the several States, as provided in the Constitution, within seven years from the date of the submission hereof to the States by the Congress.

Amendment 22 - Presidential Term Limits. <u>Ratified</u> 2/27/1951.

1. No person shall be elected to the office of the President more than twice, and no person who has held the office of President, or acted as President, for more than two years of a term to which some other person was elected President shall be elected to the office of the President more than once. But this Article shall not apply to any person holding the office of President, when this Article was proposed by the Congress, and shall not prevent any person who may be holding the office of President, or acting as President, during the term within which this Article becomes operative from holding the office of President or acting as President during the remainder of such term.

2. This article shall be inoperative unless it shall have been ratified as an amendment to the Constitution by the legislatures of three-fourths of the several States within seven years from the date of its submission to the States by the Congress.

Amendment 23 - Presidential Vote for District of Columbia. Ratified 3/29/1961.

1. The District constituting the seat of Government of the United States shall appoint in such manner as the Congress may direct: A number of electors of President and Vice President equal to the whole number of Senators and Representatives in Congress to which the District would be entitled if it were a State, but in no event more than the least populous State; they shall be in addition to those appointed by the States, but they shall be considered, for the purposes of the election of President and Vice President, to be electors appointed by a State; and they shall meet in the District and perform such duties as provided by the twelfth article of amendment.
2. The Congress shall have power to enforce this article by appropriate legislation.

Amendment 24 - Poll Tax Barred. Ratified 1/23/1964.

1. The right of citizens of the United States to vote in any primary or other election for President or Vice President, for electors for President or Vice President, or for Senator or Representative in Congress, shall not be denied or

abridged by the United States or any State by reason of failure to pay any poll tax or other tax.
2. The Congress shall have power to enforce this article by appropriate legislation.

Amendment 25 - Presidential Disability and Succession. Ratified 2/10/1967.

1. In case of the removal of the President from office or of his death or resignation, the Vice President shall become President.
2. Whenever there is a vacancy in the office of the Vice President, the President shall nominate a Vice President who shall take office upon confirmation by a majority vote of both Houses of Congress.
3. Whenever the President transmits to the President pro tempore of the Senate and the Speaker of the House of Representatives his written declaration that he is unable to discharge the powers and duties of his office, and until he transmits to them a written declaration to the contrary, such powers and duties shall be discharged by the Vice President as Acting President.
4. Whenever the Vice President and a majority of either the principal officers of the executive departments or of such other body as Congress may by law provide, transmit to the President pro tempore of the Senate and the Speaker of the House of Representatives their written declaration that the President is unable to discharge the powers and duties of his office, the Vice President shall

immediately assume the powers and duties of the office as Acting President.

Thereafter, when the President transmits to the President pro tempore of the Senate and the Speaker of the House of Representatives his written declaration that no inability exists, he shall resume the powers and duties of his office unless the Vice President and a majority of either the principal officers of the executive department or of such other body as Congress may by law provide, transmit within four days to the President pro tempore of the Senate and the Speaker of the House of Representatives their written declaration that the President is unable to discharge the powers and duties of his office. Thereupon Congress shall decide the issue, assembling within forty eight hours for that purpose if not in session. If the Congress, within twenty one days after receipt of the latter written declaration, or, if Congress is not in session, within twenty one days after Congress is required to assemble, determines by two thirds vote of both Houses that the President is unable to discharge the powers and duties of his office, the Vice President shall continue to discharge the same as Acting President; otherwise, the President shall resume the powers and duties of his office.

Amendment 26 - Voting Age Set to 18 Years. Ratified 7/1/1971.

1. The right of citizens of the United States, who are eighteen years of age or older, to vote shall not be denied

or abridged by the United States or by any State on account of age.

2. The Congress shall have power to enforce this article by appropriate legislation.

Amendment 27 - Limiting Congressional Pay Increases. Ratified 5/7/1992.

No law, varying the compensation for the services of the Senators and Representatives, shall take effect, until an election of Representatives shall have intervened.

BUY A SHARE OF THE FUTURE IN YOUR COMMUNITY

These certificates make great holiday, graduation and birthday gifts that can be personalized with the recipient's name. The cost of one S.H.A.R.E. or one square foot is $54.17. The personalized certificate is suitable for framing and will state the number of shares purchased and the amount of each share, as well as the recipient's name. The home that you participate in "building" will last for many years and will continue to grow in value.

Here is a sample SHARE certificate:

Sample certificate shown:
HABITAT FOR HUMANITY
THIS CERTIFIES THAT
YOUR NAME HERE
HAS INVESTED IN A HOME FOR A DESERVING FAMILY
1985-2005
TWENTY YEARS OF BUILDING FUTURES IN OUR COMMUNITY ONE HOME AT A TIME
1200 SQUARE FOOT HOUSE @ $65,000 = $54.17 PER SQUARE FOOT
This certificate represents a tax deductible donation. It has no cash value.

YES, I WOULD LIKE TO HELP!
I support the work that Habitat for Humanity does and I want to be part of the excitement! As a donor, I will receive periodic updates on your construction activities but, more importantly, I know my gift will help a family in our community realize the dream of homeownership. I would like to SHARE in your efforts against substandard housing in my community! (Please print below)

PLEASE SEND ME _____ SHARES at $54.17 EACH = $ $_____

In Honor Of: _____

Occasion: (Circle One)   HOLIDAY   BIRTHDAY   ANNIVERSARY
         OTHER: _____

Address of Recipient: _____

Gift From: _____ **Donor Address:** _____

Donor Email: _____

I AM ENCLOSING A CHECK FOR $ $_____ **PAYABLE TO HABITAT FOR HUMANITY OR PLEASE CHARGE MY VISA OR MASTERCARD** *(CIRCLE ONE)*

Card Number _____ Expiration Date: _____

Name as it appears on Credit Card _____ Charge Amount $ _____

Signature _____

Billing Address _____

Telephone # Day _____ Eve _____

PLEASE NOTE: Your contribution is tax-deductible to the fullest extent allowed by law.
Habitat for Humanity • P.O. Box 1443 • Newport News, VA 23601 • 757-596-5553
www.HelpHabitatforHumanity.org